# A Handcrafted Life

# A Handcrafted
# Life

### Creating a Sustainable Cottage Sanctuary

RIZZOLI
NEW YORK

TIFFANY FRANCIS-BAKER

A Handcrafted Life:
Creating A Sustainable Cottage Sanctuary
Text by Tiffany Francis-Baker

First published in Great Britain in 2023 as
"The Cottage Life: The Escapist's Guide to Cottagecore"
by Quarto Press

This book was conceived, designed, and produced by
Quintessence Editions, an imprint of The Quarto Group
6 Blundell Street, London N7 9BH

Publisher **Lorraine Dickey**
Associate Publisher **Eszter Karpati**
Senior Editor **Emma Harverson**
Assistant Editor **Ella Whiting**
Designer **Helen Bratby**
Art Director **Gemma Wilson**
Senior Art Editor **Rachel Cross**
Illustrator **Elin Manon**

First published in the United States of America in 2023
by Rizzoli International Publications, Inc.
300 Park Avenue South
New York, NY 10010
www.rizzoliusa.com

**For Rizzoli**
Publisher **Charles Miers**
Editor **Klaus Kirschbaum**
Assistant Editor **Meredith Johnson**
Managing Editor **Lynn Scrabis**

ISBN: 978-0-8478-9927-2
Library of Congress Control Number: 2022949165

2023 2024 2025 2026/ 10 9 8 7 6 5 4 3 2 1

Printed in China

**Visit us online:**
Facebook.com/RizzoliNewYork
Twitter: @Rizzoli_Books
Instagram.com/RizzoliBooks
Pinterest.com/RizzoliBooks
Youtube.com/user/RizzoliNY
Issuu.com/Rizzoli

MIX
Paper from
responsible sources
FSC
www.fsc.org
FSC® C016973

# Contents

# Introducing cottagecore

"Cottagecore reflects our collective desire to escape the chaos of modern existence: to live with more purpose, more compassion, and more joy."

I F MORE OF US VALUED FOOD AND CHEER AND SONG ABOVE HOARDED gold, it would be a merrier world." So said *The Hobbit*'s Thorin Oakenshield, as he came to the end of his life, and so begins this book about slow and simple living, inspired by the magical world of cottagecore. On the surface, cottagecore is a fashion aesthetic popularized by millennials and generation Z: an Instagrammable wonderland of floaty dresses, straw hats, and perfectly positioned coffee cups. Yet, a closer look reveals something much richer. Beneath the hashtags and filters, cottagecore reflects our collective desire to escape the chaos of modern existence: to live with more purpose, more compassion, and more joy.

To follow the cottagecore aesthetic is to wear secondhand clothes that tell their own stories; to bake fresh bread and cakes, no matter how wonky the outcome; to spend time in nature, to observe and draw the plants, to breathe fresh air, and to connect with species beyond our own. It is taking the time to notice the seasons change, or to turn off your screen mindfully and pick up an old novel instead. It is lighting a fire on the first cool night of fall and sipping a fresh cup of tea by the hearth, or watching the first spring leaves unfurl after the long, dark winter. Celebrating the small joys in life, from the first birdsong of the morning to the taste of ripe plums on a summer afternoon. And, above all else, it is learning to slow down, connect with the world around you, and be a more compassionate, conscientious citizen of the earth.

The threads of cottagecore can be traced as far back as the Ancient Greeks and the utopian land they named Arcadia, an uncorrupted place of pastoral beauty, inhabited by shepherds,

nymphs, and druids, who lived in harmony with nature. Cottagecore draws on these same values of beauty and simplicity. Fortunately for most, possession of a country cottage is not essential to embody the cottagecore spirit. It is simply a rose-tinted celebration of the smallest joys in life, if we only choose to see them: warm bread, fresh from the oven, a jug of garden flowers on the kitchen table, a comfortable dress paired with a velvet ribbon, a handwritten letter, a handmade quilt, or a bowl of glistening blackberries beside an early evening fire.

The roots of cottagecore can be found in the 1960s and '70s, when the counterculture movement emerged, driven primarily by a belief in peace over war. This birth of "hippie culture" drew on environmentally conscious projects and ideas, rural communes, thrifted furniture, and comforting, cozy interior spaces, still celebrated today for their paisley and nature-inspired patterns. The modern incarnation of cottagecore later developed throughout the 2010s, mainly through online forums and communities, while the name itself first appeared on Tumblr in 2018. During the COVID-19 pandemic, in 2020, the movement gained further traction in response to mass quarantining, as well as the exodus of people from cities to more rural settings. Cottagecore became particularly popular on Pinterest and TikTok, with thousands of people sharing scenes from nature, freshly baked bread, and embroidery projects for the world to see and enjoy. According to articles in the *New Yorker* and *Vox*, living in the style of cottagecore helped participants feel more calm and relaxed amid the chaos of the pandemic, especially for those who longed for life to be a little more simple. Video games such as *Animal Crossing* further reflected this desire for a simple, idyllic existence, as well as albums such as Taylor Swift's *folklore* and *evermore*, which were visually and lyrically centered around the cottagecore ideal.

One of the reasons cottagecore has captured the hearts of so many people is because it is largely seen as a very inclusive aesthetic in terms of gender and sexuality. Standard gender norms are encouraged to be cast aside, and it has proven popular with people throughout the LGBT+ community. It has, however, also been criticized for lacking diversity and representation, particularly as the majority of cottagecore images that emerge from a Google search depict white women, even though the aesthetic is embraced by people of all ethnicities and backgrounds. Another criticism has been whether those who practice cottagecore are idealizing rural life without recognizing the struggles associated with it, both in the past and present day. Living in the countryside often comes with its own form of hardship, and it would be naive to ignore these realities and focus only on the visuals. All in all, however, the cottagecore trend is generally considered to be a well-meaning and uplifting lifestyle, and one that encourages empathy and compassion to others and oneself.

While the arrival of the internet, new technology, and high-speed living has improved our lives in many ways, it has also brought a wave of mental health issues and an emphasis on productivity over contentment. Studies show that young people, especially those who have never known life offline, are struggling more than ever with poor mental health. It is this generation, too, that admit to feeling high levels of eco-anxiety around climate change and the future of our planet. With the effects of global warming unfolding before our eyes, it is impossible to ignore the gravity of the situation we face as a civilization and as a planet. Is it any wonder, therefore, that followers of cottagecore also value sustainability, community, and a deep connection with nature? Many who have been struck by the cottagecore trend are also passionate about living more harmoniously with each other, and with our surroundings, rejecting excessive consumerism in favor of small, simple joys. For many, it is more than a fashion trend or social media bandwagon. It is a peaceful protest against the darker elements of modern life—a gentle embrace with the past, to truly enjoy the present and nurture a brighter future.

# Chapter One

# The joy of slowing down

H OW MANY TIMES DO WE HEAR PEOPLE TALK ABOUT TIME
flying by? Many believe that the older we get, the faster life
passes—but is this really true? Some theoretical physicists
claim that time is an illusion whose flow doesn't match up with
physical reality. In other words, the concept of time may be all in our
heads, which means we can change the way we experience it. Think
back to life as a small child, when a three-hour birthday party flew by
in an instant. Thirty years later, those same three hours can feel like
a week if we are sitting in an office, longing to log off. The mind is a
powerful thing, and the truth is that life does not need to feel like it's
speeding by at all. We must simply learn to slow down.

The idea of living in the moment has been celebrated by many
philosophies and religions throughout history, but now there are
scientific studies proving its benefits. In 2010, Matthew Killingsworth
and Daniel Gilbert, psychologists at Harvard University, studied a
group of volunteers to find out how often they were focused on what
they were doing in the moment, and whether it made them happy.
They concluded that the act of reminiscing, thinking ahead, or
daydreaming tended to make the participants more miserable—even
if they were thinking about something positive. Killingsworth, the lead
author of the study, explained why this might be:

"Human beings have this unique ability to focus on things that aren't happening right now. That allows them to reflect on the past and learn from it; it allows them to anticipate and plan for the future; and it allows them to imagine things that might never occur. At the same time, it seems that human beings often use this ability in ways that are not productive and, furthermore, can be destructive to our happiness."

Living in the moment might be easier said than done, but it doesn't help that modern life has glorified being busy. In the Western world, especially, we are taught from a young age to be productive, work hard, and fill our days with meetings, extra-curricular activities, and social events. We all want to succeed in life and find contentment, but is it time we reevaluate what success really means? We spend so much time rushing around and "achieving" things that we are unable to take a step back and savor each moment. In fact, the idea of doing nothing has become completely stigmatized. Yet, what happens when we choose to pause—to slow down, take a breath, look around, and absorb the life that flows so beautifully around us? These are some of the core ideals of the cottagecore lifestyle—taking note of the present and learning to appreciate a simple life, lived right here in the moment.

# Mindfulness and breathwork

"Stop, look around at the world,
 and see the beauty beneath the bustle."

I N THE WORLD OF COTTAGECORE, LIFE REVOLVES AROUND A SIMPLE, mindful existence. We can take joy from a long afternoon with our nose in a book, a spring weekend planting seedlings, or three hours in the kitchen baking a slow loaf of sourdough. The more we are able to slow down, the more we can stop, look around at the world, and see the beauty beneath the bustle. There is so much for us to learn from the gentle pace of nature—for as Lao Tzu once said, "Nature does not hurry, yet everything is accomplished."

One simple way to start slowing our minds and bodies down is to focus on our breathing, particularly deep breathing. We take more than eight million breaths per year, but very few of them would be considered deep. In fact, deep or "diaphragmatic" breathing is one of four types of breath we might take on a regular day. All of these types of breathing are built into us, helping us to cope with daily life or interpret signals around us. Yet, deep breathing is the only one proven to have a huge number of health benefits, including helping with anxiety, depression, managing stress, improving focus, better sleep, and faster recovery from exercise.

# 5...4...3...2...1... technique

One technique that we can use to start slowing our minds, known as the **5...4...3...2...1... technique**, can also be useful for calming anxiety attacks. It is a great way to start training our brains to relax and observe the world around us, and it is easily manageable even for those with the busiest lifestyles. The first step is to look around you and name five things you can see, then four things you can feel, three you can hear, two you can smell, and, finally, one you can taste. How does it feel to exist in this moment? What does it feel like to be your unique and wonderful self? Slowing down is about recognizing the magic of our own existence and letting go of the pressure to race through life when we don't need to.

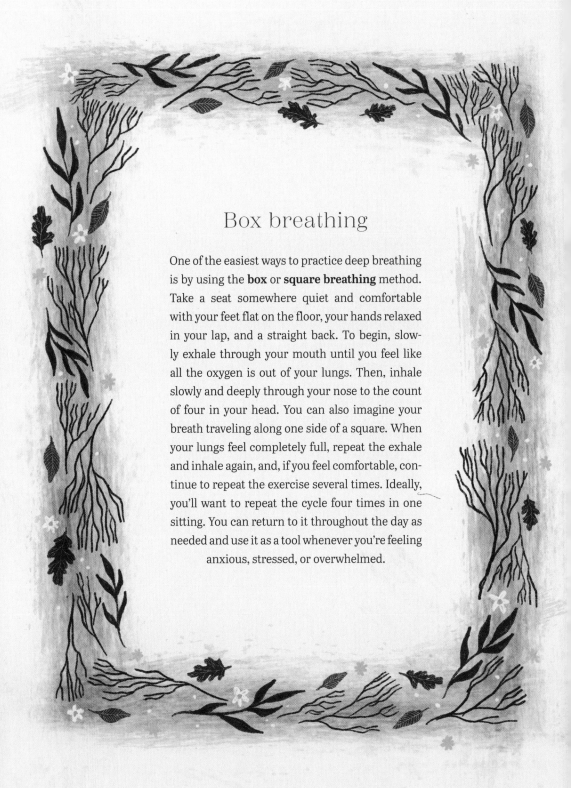

# Box breathing

One of the easiest ways to practice deep breathing is by using the **box** or **square breathing** method. Take a seat somewhere quiet and comfortable with your feet flat on the floor, your hands relaxed in your lap, and a straight back. To begin, slowly exhale through your mouth until you feel like all the oxygen is out of your lungs. Then, inhale slowly and deeply through your nose to the count of four in your head. You can also imagine your breath traveling along one side of a square. When your lungs feel completely full, repeat the exhale and inhale again, and, if you feel comfortable, continue to repeat the exercise several times. Ideally, you'll want to repeat the cycle four times in one sitting. You can return to it throughout the day as needed and use it as a tool whenever you're feeling anxious, stressed, or overwhelmed.

# The body scan

Another useful technique is known as the **body scan**, which is great for aiding relaxation, feeling fully present in your body, and helping you drift off to sleep. It involves scanning your body for any signs of tension, then "releasing" them, so that you can relax and fall asleep. Think of it like a mental x-ray for your body—one that has been scientifically proven to improve sleep, relieve anxiety and stress, increase self-compassion, and enhance self-awareness. To start, get cozy by lying down somewhere warm and comfortable—you can do it in bed to induce sleep—and follow these simple steps:

1. Focus on relaxing your body as you begin to inhale and exhale.

2. Feel the floor or bed underneath your body, and acknowledge how it is supporting you as you continue to breathe and relax.

3. Starting at the crown of your head, visualize each part of your body as you begin to move slowly down, identifying spots that feel tense. Keep breathing, and focus on relaxing tense muscles.

4. Once you have reached your toes, continue to focus on your breath, and allow yourself to drift off or relax further. If it helps, you can repeat a soft mantra such as "sleep," "breathe," or "peace."

# Digital detoxing

"You have the power to take a break, switch off, and reset your relationship with technology."

FOR MANY OF US, BEING CONNECTED AND ENGAGED WITH THE digital world is a part of everyday life. It is no longer strange to shudder at the thought of being separated from our devices—and this isn't our fault. Gadgets, apps, and social media platforms are designed to be addictive, so it will come as no surprise that many of us feel a strong attachment to them. According to research from the Nielsen Company, the average US adult spends around eleven hours each day listening to, watching, reading, or interacting with digital media in some form. While the digital world brings us plenty of joy, social connection, entertainment, and cultural value, few people can claim not to have felt the negative effects too.

So, whether you simply want to enjoy time offline without distractions, or you feel as if you have a behavioral addiction to your device, there are plenty of reasons to give digital detoxing a go. For one thing, research suggests that our constant need to keep checking emails, texts, and social media notifications is now leading to "tech stress," while heavy technology use has been associated with an increased mental health risk, particularly among younger people. Devices are also responsible for disrupting our sleep quality and quantity, with studies showing that the use of social media in bed at night increases the likelihood of anxiety, insomnia, and shorter sleep duration. Throw in the issues surrounding productivity and distraction, comparison and self-esteem, as well as major FOMO (fear of missing out) when we see others' highlight reels on Instagram, and it's no wonder these new technologies have their downside.

**When to take a break**
Not everyone needs to take a break from their devices, but if you are experiencing any of the following symptoms, you might enjoy a digital detox:

→ You feel anxious or stressed when you can't find your cell phone.
→ You feel compelled to check your cell phone every few minutes, even when you haven't received any notifications.
→ You feel depressed, anxious, or angry after scrolling through social media feeds.
→ You are preoccupied with how your posts are performing on social media.
→ You are worried you'll miss out on something if you don't check your device regularly.
→ Your use of technology is regularly disrupting your sleep pattern.
→ You have trouble focusing on a task without being distracted by your cell phone.

If you experience any of these issues, you are certainly not alone. The good news is you have the power to take a break, switch off, and reset your relationship with technology.

# How to detox

A digital detox isn't meant to be miserable, even though it may feel like it from time to time! The aim is to improve your overall wellbeing, but remember to be compassionate and forgiving if you slip up. There is no right or wrong way to do it, and it is not your fault if you are addicted to something that was designed to be addictive. Follow the steps below to experiment with what you can manage, and recognize any of the benefits that come your way as a good result.

### STEP 1: Be realistic

By all means, if you are in a position to fully ditch your devices for a few days, weeks, or months, it might be worth a go. Some of us have never lived in a world without digital technology, while for others it is a distant memory, so, if you are able to recreate that experience today, it could be incredibly liberating and refreshing.

For many of us, however, disconnecting completely is not possible. Even if we dislike social media or don't watch Netflix, most of us use phone-based messaging systems to stay in touch with friends and family. It is also likely that we require emails and digital software to carry out our day-to-day jobs, and we can't expect our bosses to understand if we just stop reading our emails. Instead, the key is to take control over when we are using our devices and when we are choosing not to engage with them—to feel the urge to pick up our devices, but to resist, and focus on the real world.

STEP 2: **Set boundaries**

Sit down and work out what is realistic for your life—whether it's deciding a window of working hours, an hourly limit to your screen time, or taking a temporary break from addictive apps and social media platforms. One of the easiest ways to start is to designate your evenings as technology-free time, if possible. Get creative with other ways to spend your time—start a new hobby, meet with friends, or go on a date night. You can experiment with things such as using airplane mode or keeping your phone in another room to see whether they help reduce your overall device use. The most important thing is being in control of your technology, rather than allowing it to control you.

STEP 3: **Unlearn your habits**

Technology has become so integrated into our lives—for good and bad—that it is sometimes difficult to imagine a scenario without it. Yet, there are always ways to unlearn habits and rethink your day-to-day routines, reducing your reliance on technology and finding new ways to do the things you love. Here are some easy ways to get started:

→ Avoid taking your devices into your bedroom, if you can help it. Invest in a regular alarm clock. You are guaranteed a better night's sleep, and you'll soon kick the wake-up-and-check addiction.

→ Put your devices away when enjoying hobbies such as reading or crafting. If you need to look something up, you can use it as a chance to stretch your legs and walk to your cell phone.

→ Use recipe books instead of looking up cooking ideas online.

→ Play an entire album or playlist rather than individual songs so you don't have to keep tinkering with Spotify.

→ Turn off push notifications on your cell phone. This means you have to intentionally open an app to see your messages, rather than being sucked in when you might not want to be.

→ If you need to manage social media accounts for work or play, try setting time aside each day to carry out your tasks. One technique is to have a window in the morning for creating content and another in the afternoon for responding to engagement.

# Self-care, habits, and rituals

"New habits don't have to be life changing;
consistency is far more important."

ARE YOU AWARE OF YOUR DAILY HABITS? DO THEY NURTURE YOUR mind, body, and soul, or are they holding you back? A recent study by the American Psychological Association revealed that around 45 percent of our activities in a given day are habitual, performed automatically without much conscious thought. This statistic proves how easy it is to form habits, which shape our everyday actions for better or worse, without even knowing it.

By definition, good habits are a series of events: we recognize a cue, create a positive response, and receive a consistent reward every time. For example, we might hear our alarm clock go off at sunrise, motivate ourselves to get out of bed straight away, and enjoy the rewards of rising early. It is easy to see how good habits can turn to bad ones, especially if we start associating those cues with actions that are less healthy or productive. But it is also within our control to turn negative habits into positive ones. Even better, we can create brand new habits altogether to improve different aspects of our lifestyle.

New habits don't have to be life changing; consistency is far more important. You'll be amazed at how quickly lots of little positive moments can affect your day-to-day life. Be intentional with the habits you would like to focus on and realistic with what you can manage. Celebrate the small victories, and don't get caught up in being "perfect."

The following habits and rituals can be slotted into your daily routine and are perfect for slowing down, observing the world around you, and savoring every moment of your day.

# The morning kettle ritual

For many of us, the first thing that swims into our sleepy minds when
we wake is to make that first cup of hot tea or coffee to start the day.
Yet, do we really savor it and give it the time it deserves, or do we rush
through it amid the chaos of an early morning? Making time to enjoy
your first cup, even if it's just five minutes each morning, can make
a huge difference to how the rest of your day pans out. You can tailor
your own ritual to suit your tastes and routine.

→ Think about your favorite "first drink"
of the day, and make sure you're treating
yourself to the best version it can be. Do
you prefer instant coffee or fresh beans;
breakfast tea or fruity blends; teabags or
loose leaves? Conjure up your ultimate
morning cup and indulge in it.

→ Be mindful of the whole process, from
boiling the water to steeping the leaves.
These simple tasks can bring the most joy.

→ Combine your morning cup with
something else you enjoy. Read a page of
your book, play your favorite song, listen
to the birds singing in the garden, or
enjoy some gentle stretches.

→ Use all your senses to enjoy your
morning cup. What does your coffee
smell like? How did the water sound as it
bubbled and boiled? Which mug did you
choose this morning, and why?

# The brain dump

You've turned off your screen, dimmed the lights,
taken a shower, and read your book—the perfect recipe
for a good night's sleep! Except that sometimes our brains just
don't want to cooperate. Have you ever felt your thoughts start
to go crazy as soon as your head hits the pillow? Perhaps you're
processing events from earlier in the day, or playing out a conversation
you wish you'd had, or even just whizzing through work ideas? There's
nothing more frustrating than feeling as if your brain is partying when all
you want to do is sleep, which is why you might like to consider introducing
a brain dump to your evening routine.

Brain dumping is simply grabbing a notebook and writing down all the
thoughts that are whizzing through your head—the good ones and the
silly ones—so that they can be put to rest and forgotten about until the
next morning. Not only does this help calm a busy brain, but also it
allows you to take abstract ideas and turn them into something
more tangible when you return to the page the next morning.
Try not to worry about neatness, spelling, or grammar—
just get those thoughts down so you can get back to
your precious sleep, guilt-free.

# The seasonal space

Did you know that in the world of the occult, witches are known to have special altars and sacred spaces in which to cast spells, meditate, and celebrate the changing seasons? Whether or not you believe in magic, the idea of observing the seasons and gathering treasures throughout the year is a great one, and can help ground us in the here and now, while also bringing the beauty of the outside world in. Our bodies and energy levels are naturally responsive to what is happening around us, so you can use a seasonal space as a way to tap into how you're really feeling. In winter, we might feel cold and tired, and we should allow ourselves time to rest; spring wakes us up and inspires us to start afresh; summer is the season of productivity, joy, and full energy; fall allows us to return to earth and retreat back into ourselves once again.

To set up your own seasonal space, find a quiet corner of the house where the light and energy feels good to you. It could be as small as the end of a bookshelf or as big as a whole tabletop. Some people arrange their space by the fireplace, on the windowsill, or a clear corner of their office.

### Cleansing
Clean the area well, using eco-friendly materials, then think about what you would like to use this space for. Will it be for meditation, singing, journaling, spell casting, or other forms of self-care?

### Focal objects
You might like to feature a central object or image to focus on, such as an art print, a trinket or sculpture, or a plant. Other objects that lend themselves to sacred spaces include candles and wax melts, precious stones and crystals, incense burners, fresh flowers, and photographs.

### Embracing nature
Most importantly, try to decorate your altar with the outside world in mind. Which season is passing at the moment? Which plants and flowers are growing? Which colors represent the natural world at this time? How does this time of year make you feel?

# The new moon bath

Do you follow the cycles of the moon? Observing the lunar phases is not only a great way to form a deeper connection with nature's rhythms, but can also be used as a template for our own energy and creativity. Each phase of the cycle is thought to inspire a different type of energy. The new moon is the start of a new cycle of opportunity; a time for setting intentions for the coming month, as we think about what we want to create, the projects we have been putting off, or simply some positive changes we would like to embrace.

A new moon bath is the perfect way to start a new lunar cycle; a relaxing, mindful moment to ourselves, in which we can meditate on past, present, and future, and think clearly about the path forward. Your new moon bath can take any shape, but here is an evening ritual to get you started:

1. No matter the season, open the window wide so that, if possible, you can see the night sky and breathe in fresh air.

2. Run your bath to your preferred temperature—around 98°F (37°C) is perfect, as it's hot enough to create steam but not so hot that you'll feel uncomfortable or flushed.

3. Use a bath salt blend to infuse the water with nourishing goodness. Try the lavender bath salt recipe in chapter 2 (see page 53).

4. While the bath is running, make yourself a drink. It is best to avoid caffeine and alcohol before bed, so try a relaxing, clarifying herbal tea blend such as peppermint, oat flower, chamomile, valerian, or licorice root.

5. Turn down the lights, and light a candle or wax-melt burner.

6. Choose an intention to meditate on during your bath. What would you like to achieve this month? What are your priorities? What will bring you closer to contentment? How can you help others along the way?

7. Allow yourself to soak in the bath for 15–20 minutes, then use an exfoliating scrub to buff your skin, washing away the old to make way for the new.

8. Dry yourself with a clean, soft towel and slip away to bed, holding your intentions softly in your mind.

# Chapter Two

# The joy of making

HUMANS HAVE ALWAYS BEEN ARTISTS AND CRAFTERS. FROM ancient, charcoal-scratched drawings on cave walls to 3D digital printing and everything in between, we are creative souls who love nothing more than to make, shape, color, and discover.

The act of making and crafting is not only fun, it has proven scientific benefits for our wellbeing. Research published by University College London shows that engaging with the visual arts can reduce anxiety and stress. Learning a craft is associated with an overall increase in wellbeing and mood, due to the effort, multisensory engagement, repetitive actions, and anticipation of satisfaction that comes with making something. Creative activities also require focus and attention, which act as a form of meditation, keeping participants' minds present in the moment.

The benefits of craft extend beyond ourselves too. Otherwise known as the art of gentle protest, the term "craftivism" has been coined to describe how art can be used to drive positive change. For if we want our world to be more beautiful, kind, and fair, asks online community group the Craftivist Collective, couldn't we make our activism more beautiful, kind, and fair too? Craftivism could include anything from community "stitch-ins" outside train stations to designing miniature banners, embroidering eco-slogans, organizing postcard campaigns, and knitting anti-war tokens. Whether you want to make a difference from the comfort of your own home, or you're looking for like-minded communities to join, craftivism is a wonderful way to use your creativity for the greater good. Studies have also shown that those who gather together for communal crafting are able to cope better with social anxiety and depression, and experience reduced loneliness and isolation.

The best thing about the wide variety of arts and crafts on offer today is that there is always something to suit everyone. Even if you don't consider yourself a "creative" person, there will always be some craft or hobby that lights you up—it's just a case of finding it. Whether you only have an hour a week at your kitchen table, or you have time and money to invest in something new, getting your creative juices flowing has never been easier. Looking for ideas to get started? Try this list of beginner-friendly crafts, all of which are affordable to start with and don't require much space:

→ Knitting, crochet, and macramé
→ Cross-stitch and embroidery
→ Air-dry clay modeling
→ Wood carving
→ Découpage
→ Drawing and painting
→ Quilting and sewing
→ Calligraphy and brush lettering

# Needlework

"Essential for repairing clothes and other textiles, needlework is also an artform in itself."

W HEN WE THINK OF NEEDLEWORK, IT'S EASY TO THINK OF Jane Austen's heroines lounging around in their drawing rooms, embroidering cushions while waiting for their loved ones to propose. Yet, while needlework may seem delicate and time-consuming, in reality it is an extremely useful and versatile skill to master, as *Ladies' Needlework Penny Magazine* remarked in the Victorian era:

> *"There are many women who persuade themselves that the occupations particularly allotted to their sex are extremely frivolous; but it is one of the common errors of a depraved taste to confound simplicity with frivolity. The use of the needle is simple, but not frivolous."*

Not only is it essential for repairing clothes and other textiles, needlework is also an artform in itself when it comes to embroidery and other decorative techniques. Like all crafts, it has proven health benefits too. A study by Naomi Clarke, University of Bristol, showed that participating in sewing as a leisure activity contributed to psychological wellbeing through increased pride, enjoyment, self-awareness, and "flow," particularly in younger women. The term "needlework" is itself a broad one, encompassing a wide variety of different skills and crafts, including sewing, knitting, crochet, embroidery, cross-stitch, quilting, appliqué, lacemaking, macramé, and braiding.

# How to darn a sock

Clothes may be cheap to produce these days, but that doesn't mean
we need to throw them out when they're damaged and buy new ones.
When you choose to repair your clothes instead, it benefits your
wardrobe, your wallet, the environment, and your mental health.
The less we throw away, the less we pollute the planet, which is why
learning to make simple repairs can be so rewarding. There are several
ways to start making basic repairs, from mending hems to stitching
buttons, and sewing on patches. The easiest way to start learning is
the humble art of darning a sock—a small, simple task—and it won't
be the end of the world if it goes wrong!

**You will need:**

*Sewing needle*

*Thread—choose a color that best matches the sock*

*A darning egg—available in all good craft stores, but you can also use a tennis ball or a smooth rock*

*Sewing scissors*

1. Thread the needle with one or two strands of thread, depending on the weight of the sock. Tie a knot in the end after threading.

2. Turn the sock inside out and pull it over the darning egg (or alternative), placing the egg underneath the section you are repairing. This helps push the material of the sock out to make the hole visible.

3. Carefully trim away any ragged edges or frayed ends using your scissors.

4. Push the needle into the sock through one end of the hole and make a large running stitch to the other side of the hole. To do this, all you need to do is run your needle and thread up through the inside of the sock and out on the other side of the hole, then make a stitch to the right, and pull the needle back across the hole and up out of the other side again. Once you have covered the hole with parallel stitches, add a few rows either side of the hole, too, to reinforce your repair.

5. Next, repeat your stitches, but this time sew perpendicular to the first stitches, weaving the needle in and out of the first stitches to make the repair more sturdy.

6. Tie off the thread with a knot, and snip using your scissors.

# Embroidery

Embroidery has seen a resurgence in modern crafting, perhaps due to its simple, mindful nature and the ease with which it can be picked up and put down in small pockets of time. The aim is to decorate fabric or other materials using a needle to apply thread, but it can also incorporate beads, pearls, ribbons, or sequins, depending on the design. There are plenty of beginners' embroidery kits available online and in craft stores, or you can have a go at designing something original from scratch.

To start a basic embroidery project, you may want to buy a few inexpensive items: first, embroidery needles in sizes 1–10, which can be used for most embroidery techniques; then, a selection of embroidery threads or "floss," which consist of around six strands twisted together, usually made of cotton, silk, linen, or polyester. A pair of small scissors is useful, and it is recommended to work on a good-quality fabric with a lower thread count, such as cotton, linen, or muslin, which allows the needle to pass through more easily. An inexpensive embroidery hoop keeps the fabric taut and easier to work with, as well as providing a simple frame for the finished piece.

To get you started, five basic embroidery stitches can be combined to create simple yet beautiful designs: running stitch, useful for outlining designs; satin stitch, handy for filling shapes with solid, smooth stitches; stem stitch, often used to create flowers, vines, or anything curved; back stitch, which creates a continuous line; and French knot, which is used for decoration.

# Patchwork quilts

Patchwork quilts are deceptively simple to make and a wonderful way to use up scraps of fabric. They are also a lovely way to reuse sentimental fabrics such as loved ones' clothes; any fabric with a memory of its own can be sewn into a quilt and treasured forever as a family heirloom. Quilting is a mindful, methodical way to get started with sewing, and once you've mastered the traditional square design, you'll have the basic skills to think of more adventurous themes, including geometric shapes, historical scenes, and landscapes. Making a patchwork quilt requires two separate skills—patchworking and quilting. Patchworking is the art of sewing together pieces of fabric to form a pattern or block, while quilting is the act of sewing together the three layers that make up a quilt—the top, central wadding, and backing.

# Sew your own quilt

The following lap-sized quilt will measure approximately 57 x 67 in. (145 x 170 cm), and is perfect for snuggling up with on the couch. It can also be made larger by adding extra rows or columns, and you can add a border around the squares, if preferred.

**You will need:**

*42 fabric squares, around 10 in. (25 cm) wide*

*Cotton quilt wadding, at least 59 x 71 in. (150 x 180 cm). You can sew sections together if they are not in one complete piece*

*39 in. (100 cm) fabric for the outer binding*

*At least 55 x 63 in. (140 x 160 cm) backing fabric (again, you can sew sections together if they are not in one complete piece)*

*Cotton thread*

*Sewing machine*

*Pins*

*Rotary cutter*

*Self-healing mat*

*Quilting ruler*

1. Check that your squares are neatly cut with no jagged or frayed edges, then lay them out on a large table or clean floor to decide on your design. Arrange the squares in seven rows and six columns according to preference. If using a border, add one by measuring and cutting out strips of fabric and laying them alongside the outer edges of the squares. Once you are happy with the design, pin the squares together in rows.

2. Using your sewing machine, stitch the squares in each row together by sewing a line ¼ in. (5 mm) from the edge of each square (this is called the seam allowance).

3. Once the rows are complete, start stitching each row together until you have a completed quilt top layer. At this point, add the border if you have decided to use one.

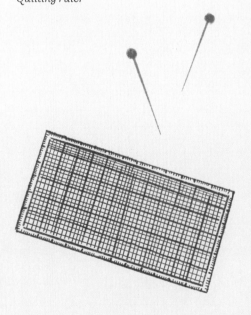

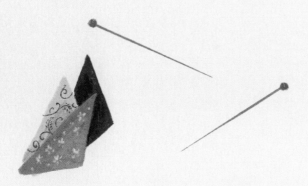

4. Quilt the layers together using your sewing machine. You want to create a consistent stitch running all over the fabric that will pull the three layers together. Pin the layers together first, then either use a basic straight stitch or look online for more decorative ideas. Sandwich together the backing fabric, interior wadding, and top patchwork fabric, making sure the decorative sides are both facing outwards, away from the wadding inside.

5. Finally, finish the quilt by neatening up any scrappy edges using scissors. Then cut a narrow strip of fabric that will act as your binding, sealing the sides of the quilt together so you can't see inside the quilted layers. Sew the binding fabric along each of the four sides using a straight stitch ¼ in. (5 mm) from the edge, as with the individual squares.

## Tips

→ Most craft stores sell cheap bundles of fabric called "fat quarters," which are perfect for patchworking.

→ Take a photo of your layout before you start sewing or you may forget which squares go where.

→ If cutting your own squares out of fabric, use a cardboard template to draw around rather than measuring every time. It will produce a more consistent shape and save you a lot of hassle!

→ If you don't enjoy pinning, you could invest in water-soluble glue to stick squares together, which will then dissolve in the wash.

→ Quilting is a very forgiving craft, so don't worry if you make a few mistakes or measure up a bit wrong. It's all part of the process and won't make the quilt any less beautiful!

# Flower power

"These beautiful, fragile blooms encapsulate the best
of nature, which is why they have been our muses
in art, craft, and literature for thousands of years."

IN HER NOVEL *THE SECRET GARDEN*, FRANCES HODGSON BURNETT observed that "if you look the right way, you can see that the whole world is a garden." Nothing proves this more than the simple joy of watching plants grow and flowers bloom, even on the darkest, stormiest of days. People have always been drawn to flowers and the symbolism behind them. The Victorians even wrote books about the language of flowers—how giving a posy to your lover came loaded with secret messages, all depending on which flowers you included in the bunch. In the 1960s, flowers were used to protest war and advocate for peace and love. And is it any wonder? These beautiful, fragile blooms encapsulate the best of nature, which is why they have been our muses in art, craft, and literature for thousands of years. Their abundance and willingness to grow are what make flowers so enjoyable to work with. So, here are a few ideas to get you started on a crafty, floriographical journey of your own.

# Flower arranging

Arranging flowers might seem intimidating if you don't know where to begin, but the magic of flowers lies in the fact that a single stem is as beautiful as an entire vaseful, so start small and relish in the delight of a simple floral display, shaped by your own hands. The basics of flower arranging focus on color, texture, fragrance, height, width, and symmetry. Are you drawn to muted, earthy tones or bright pops of color? Do you like sleek, minimalist blossoms, or busy, frilly, papery ones? How tall would you like your arrangement? What kind of smells would you like to include? These are all great questions to explore as you learn the basics of the craft and, in the meantime, here is a simple technique for putting together your own mason jar arrangement for the kitchen table.

**You will need:**

*Selection of seasonal flowers*
*    and greenery—of your choice!*
*Clean mason jar*
*A pair of pruning shears*
*Twine*
*Fresh water*

<br>

Tip
The best flowers are homegrown, locally sourced, and ethically produced. Be careful not to pick rare or endangered wildflowers, and try to stick to seasonal blooms when buying from suppliers, as they will have a lower carbon footprint.

1. Stand your tallest flower against the jar and cut the stem down so that it stands no higher than one and a half times the height of the jar. This will be the full height of your arrangement.

2. Start adding medium-sized flowers in groups of three, five, or seven. Rather than focusing on symmetry, group stems together so that they form "corners" in the jar. For example, you might have three roses in the middle, a cluster of five lilies to the right, and another trio of smaller flowers to the front, such as oxeye daisies or carnations. If you're adding a larger flower head, such as a hydrangea or sunflower, keep these solitary, low down, and to the side of the arrangement so that they don't block everything else out.

3. Fill the gaps with simple foliage such as fern, willow, viburnum, or periwinkle—anything seasonal and easily available. Use this to create the overall shape of your arrangement.

4. Once the greenery is in place, fill any visual gaps with the smallest flowers in your selection.

5. When you are happy with the rough composition of your arrangement, grasp it at the base and remove from the jar. Use twine to tie the stems together. You can then revisit the overall shape and trim the stems to reduce the height of individual flowers, where necessary.

6. Fill the jar with fresh water. Place the tied flowers in the jar, and finish off with any last adjustments to your arrangement.

# Floral wreaths

Fresh, floral wreaths are not just for the Christmas holidays—they can be made and used all year round in order to celebrate the cycles of nature. Not only is wreathmaking a wonderful, meditative craft to get stuck into on quiet afternoons, but wreaths are also a great way to observe the changing seasons and take note of what is growing, blossoming, ripening, and falling all around us. For this reason, the best kinds of wreaths are made of completely organic materials that can biodegrade, which means you can return nature's treasures to the earth when you have finished with them. Try experimenting with different compositions throughout the year, and have fun with where you hang your wreath too. While doorways are traditional, you could also try adorning your walls, hanging them over mantels, or even placing them around your garden.

## Seasonal wreath ideas

*Spring:* eucalyptus, fern, myrtle, willow, olive leaves

*Summer:* rose, forsythia, blueberries, lavender, seashells

*Fall:* pine cones, nuts, acorns, hawthorn berries, thyme, juniper

*Winter:* holly, mistletoe, dried orange slices, cinnamon sticks, cranberries

# Wildflower seed paper

If you love writing letters, wrapping gifts, or sending party invitations,
try making your own wildflower seed paper to give your local wildlife
a boost at the same time. Wildflowers are a vital source of food and
shelter for bees, butterflies, and other insects. Once you've made
and used this paper, simply pop it in the ground and watch it grow.
Try to reuse recyclable paper, such as newspaper, old printer paper,
and shreddings.

**You will need:**

*Scraps of recyclable paper*
*Blender*
*Warm water*
*A mix of native wildflower seeds*
*Flat-bottomed dish*
*Piece of muslin cloth as wide as the dish*
*Dish-washing sponge*
*Bowl*

1. Tear the paper into small pieces and add to the blender until it is half full, then add about half as much warm water. Blend to a pulp for around 20–30 seconds.
2. Sprinkle in a teaspoon of wildflower seeds and stir. Do not blend.
3. Lay the muslin cloth inside the flat-bottomed dish and pour in the pulp, flattening it out with your hands or a large spoon.
4. Once evenly spread, use the sponge to remove excess water from the pulp, draining it into the bowl.
5. When as much water as possible has been removed, carefully lift the muslin from the dish and turn the paper out onto a hard, flat surface. Leave to air dry for two days.
6. Once dry, lift the paper from the cloth and use as you wish.

# Lavender bath salts

Plants have long been celebrated for their medicinal powers. This natural recipe uses lavender flowers to create a relaxing salt-bath blend, perfect for calming the nervous system and lifting the mood. Natural salts have different mineral compositions that are released into the water as they dissolve. Epsom salts are great for muscle pain; coarse sea salt soothes achy legs and feet; Himalayan salt reduces stress; French clay salt draws out impurities from the skin. If lavender isn't your thing, you could swap the oil and flowers for rose, chamomile, or rosemary.

**You will need:**
*20 drops lavender essential oil*
*1 tablespoon (15 ml) olive oil*
*3 cups salt crystals—see above for options*
*½ cup fresh or dried lavender flower heads*
*Small mixing bowl*
*Large mixing bowl*
*Hand whisk*

1. In the small bowl, combine the lavender oil and olive oil until blended.
2. In the large bowl, combine the salt crystals and lavender flowers.
3. Pour the small bowl of oils into the large bowl, and whisk thoroughly to coat the salt crystals and flowers.
4. Transfer to an airtight container, and sprinkle liberally into a hot bath.

## Tip
To prevent the salts hardening, make sure your container is stored with the lid tightly closed.

# Working
# with wood

"Working with wood allows us to hold all of life in
our hands and transform it into something new."

THERE IS SOMETHING MAGICAL ABOUT HOLDING A PIECE OF WOOD
in your hands that was once a tree, made up of carbon, oxygen,
minerals, water, and all the passing time that allows things to
grow. It is both hard and soft, strong yet fragile, fuel and heat, life and
death. Working with wood allows us to hold all of life in our hands and
transform it into something new. Working and connecting with wood
could mean simply foraging pieces to decorate your home, or shaping
it with hand and blade. Beginners would do well to learn to sharpen
a knife, find out the difference between seasoned and green wood,
and nurture a basic understanding of what trees and plants are doing
through the seasons. The most important thing is to get outside and
immerse yourself in nature, ready to receive anything it has to offer.

# Wild wind chimes

One of the simplest nature-inspired crafts for the home is a wind chime—a collection of suspended sticks, tubes, and bells that chime as they move in the breeze. Wind chimes date back to the earliest civilizations and are often said to ward off evil spirits with their beautiful, windblown songs. The best-sounding additions to a wind chime are usually made of hollow tubes—such as copper pipes or bamboo stems—but the truth is that anything can be added for both sound and beauty. Try gathering natural materials to put together your own wind chime, tied with twine or wire and suspended from a long stick. You could even carve your own shapes into the pieces, or add other embellishments such as ribbons or beads. Hang it by your door or window, and wait for the wind to cast its spell.

**Try foraging these items to make up your wind chime:**

*Twigs and
   small branches*
*Pine cones*
*Nuts and acorns*
*Seashells*
*Cuttlefish bones*
*Driftwood*
*Pebbles*
*Snail shells*
*Tree bark*

# Willow star bunting

These eco-friendly decorations will bring rustic charm to your home all year round, or they can be interwoven with lights and ribbons at Christmas for a festive touch. Willow is prized for its flexibility, meaning it has been used for centuries to weave fences, baskets, and wreaths. It is a common species, and you only need a few stems for this craft, but if you can't find any, try looking for hazel or dogwood instead. They are best collected in the fall, just after the leaves have dropped.

**You will need:**
*Stems of willow, hazel, or dogwood,*
 *around 39 in. (1 m) each in length*
*A ball of natural twine*
*A pair of pruning shears*

1. Hold each willow stem at the thickest end, and gently bend the wood as you follow the diagram below to make your star shape.

2. When the star is complete, cross the two ends over and tie together using the twine, then snip any excess wood away using pruning shears.

3. Once you have made a few stars, measure out another piece of twine to use as your bunting string, and attach each star in a line. You can do this either by sliding them along like beads or by tying each one individually to keep them in place.

# Pyrography

They say that alchemy is the process of taking something ordinary and turning it into something extraordinary, often in a way that cannot be explained. And while there is nothing particularly mystical about the science of pyrography—using heat to burn images into wood—there is certainly a sense of magic to it. Pyrography is a centuries-old artform that was popularized in the medieval period, when blacksmiths realized they could use the hot metal from their forge to burn intricate designs onto other surfaces. If you love drawing with traditional pencils or inks, then pyrography, also known as woodburning, is one of the simplest and most affordable ways to take your drawings off the page and start exploring a new medium. The best thing about pyrography is that it's very beginner friendly. All you need is an inexpensive tool called a woodburning pen, which is available to buy online for under $40, and foraged pieces of wood or premade wooden items such as spoons and cutting boards. From simple lines to full-scale art pieces, as long as there is access to electricity, anyone can plug in and try this mesmerizing craft.

# Wood carving

Did you know that wood carving is one of the oldest art forms known to mankind? For as long as we have been sharpening blades, we have carved patterns and shapes out of wood—not only for useful tools, but also for artistic expression. The beauty of woodcarving is that once you are used to the feel of the knife and the techniques needed, this simple craft can be enjoyed at the kitchen table with no other equipment necessary. It is a craft known for its mindful and therapeutic nature, with carvers becoming absorbed in their work for hours without noticing, forgetting their stresses, and pushing unwelcome thoughts out in order to focus on the task at hand. To get started, all you need to invest in is a purpose-designed knife or two (curved knives are particularly useful for carving out the bowls of spoons).

# Carve a water talisman

All kinds of natural treasures can be found drifting on our rivers and tides. Driftwood is particularly special—a material that hardens as it floats, preserved by the water and bleached by the sun. This simple talisman can be carved out of driftwood or green (fresh) wood, and decorated with a pyrography pen to carry the water with you wherever you go.

**You will need:**
*A piece of driftwood or green (fresh) wood*
*A sharp carving knife or penknife*
*A pyrography pen*
*Sandpaper (optional)*

Tip
To protect your wood, try oiling it using a clean rag and your choice of walnut or olive oil.

1. Take your piece of wood and draw an oval-shaped pencil outline to mark out the shape of your talisman.
2. To hold your knife, tilt the top edge toward you and place your thumb along the blunt back of the blade. Keep your remaining fingers out of the way by wrapping them around the handle, and begin to carve away from your body, shaving off small pieces of wood to turn your piece of wood into a rounded shape.
3. When you are happy with the shape, you can either leave any natural bumps or use sandpaper to smooth down the whole piece.
4. Use a pencil to draw your design onto the talisman and, following the instructions for your pyrography pen, burn your design into the wood. Don't panic if you go wrong—simply sand down the surface and try again.

**Design ideas for the pyrography step:**

Aquarius symbol

Water element symbol

Moon and stars symbol

# Chapter Three

# Nurturing your home

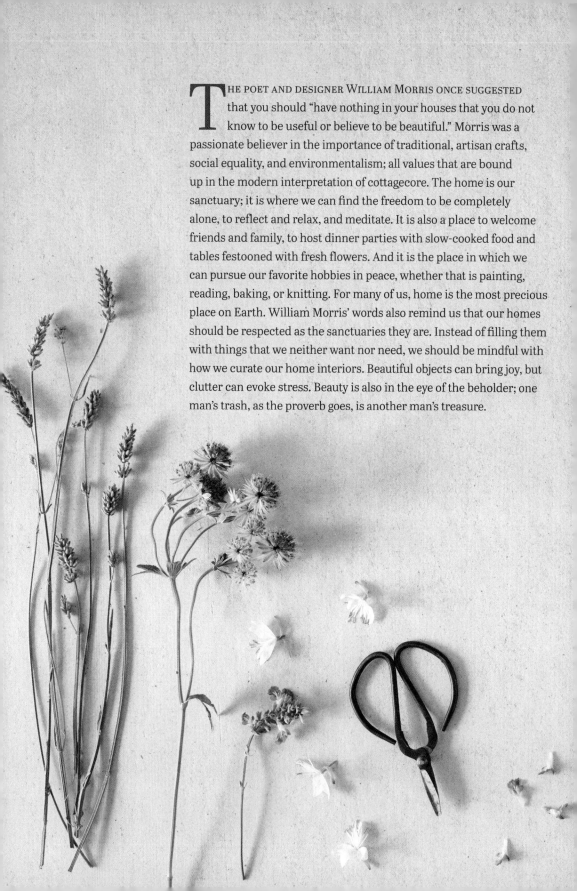

THE POET AND DESIGNER WILLIAM MORRIS ONCE SUGGESTED that you should "have nothing in your houses that you do not know to be useful or believe to be beautiful." Morris was a passionate believer in the importance of traditional, artisan crafts, social equality, and environmentalism; all values that are bound up in the modern interpretation of cottagecore. The home is our sanctuary; it is where we can find the freedom to be completely alone, to reflect and relax, and meditate. It is also a place to welcome friends and family, to host dinner parties with slow-cooked food and tables festooned with fresh flowers. And it is the place in which we can pursue our favorite hobbies in peace, whether that is painting, reading, baking, or knitting. For many of us, home is the most precious place on Earth. William Morris' words also remind us that our homes should be respected as the sanctuaries they are. Instead of filling them with things that we neither want nor need, we should be mindful with how we curate our home interiors. Beautiful objects can bring joy, but clutter can evoke stress. Beauty is also in the eye of the beholder; one man's trash, as the proverb goes, is another man's treasure.

In the world of cottagecore, the clue is in the name: the aim for many is to recreate the cozy, rural aesthetic of an old-fashioned cottage. But what exactly is a cottage? The word comes from England's feudal period, when a landowner would have given their worker a small house with enough garden to feed themselves and their family. Over time, the word "cottage" simply became the name for a small house, or even a larger house that was built for practicality over spectacle, such as Jane Austen's cottage in Chawton, England. Yet the word never lost its original association with modest country life, a self-sustaining sanctuary for those who lived within it. Few of us have medieval cottages with acres of garden these days, but that doesn't mean we can't capture the magic of the past within our modern homes. All that matters is a focus on beauty, usefulness, comfort, and craftsmanship. No matter where we live, our backgrounds, or how much money we have, the cottage is a place for everyone.

# Interiors

"Stories can exist in a single candle flame
or jar of cut flowers."

H OW DO YOU CAPTURE THE MAGIC OF A SIMPLE COTTAGE? And how do you bring it to life within the context of the modern world? Cottagecore is all about the unique mixture of old and new, as well as the particular connection each person has to their home and belongings. A cottagecore home could involve an eclectic mix of antique furniture, flagstone floors, and open fires, or it could simply be full of cozy throws and cushions, candles, and books. There is no right or wrong way to do it, but the aim is to tell stories through your home. Who sits in this corner by the window, reading books and looking out across the garden? Who kneads dough at this wooden kitchen table, and how many cups of coffee have been poured from this old kettle? Stories can exist in a single candle flame or jar of cut flowers. You don't need to spend lots of money to create your cottagecore look either. The internet has made it easier than ever to find secondhand bargains on Facebook or eBay, while thrift stores, flea markets, and vintage fairs are all treasure troves for curating the perfect collection of items for your home. Look for things that are well-made and built to last, especially those more traditional pieces that will never go out of style.

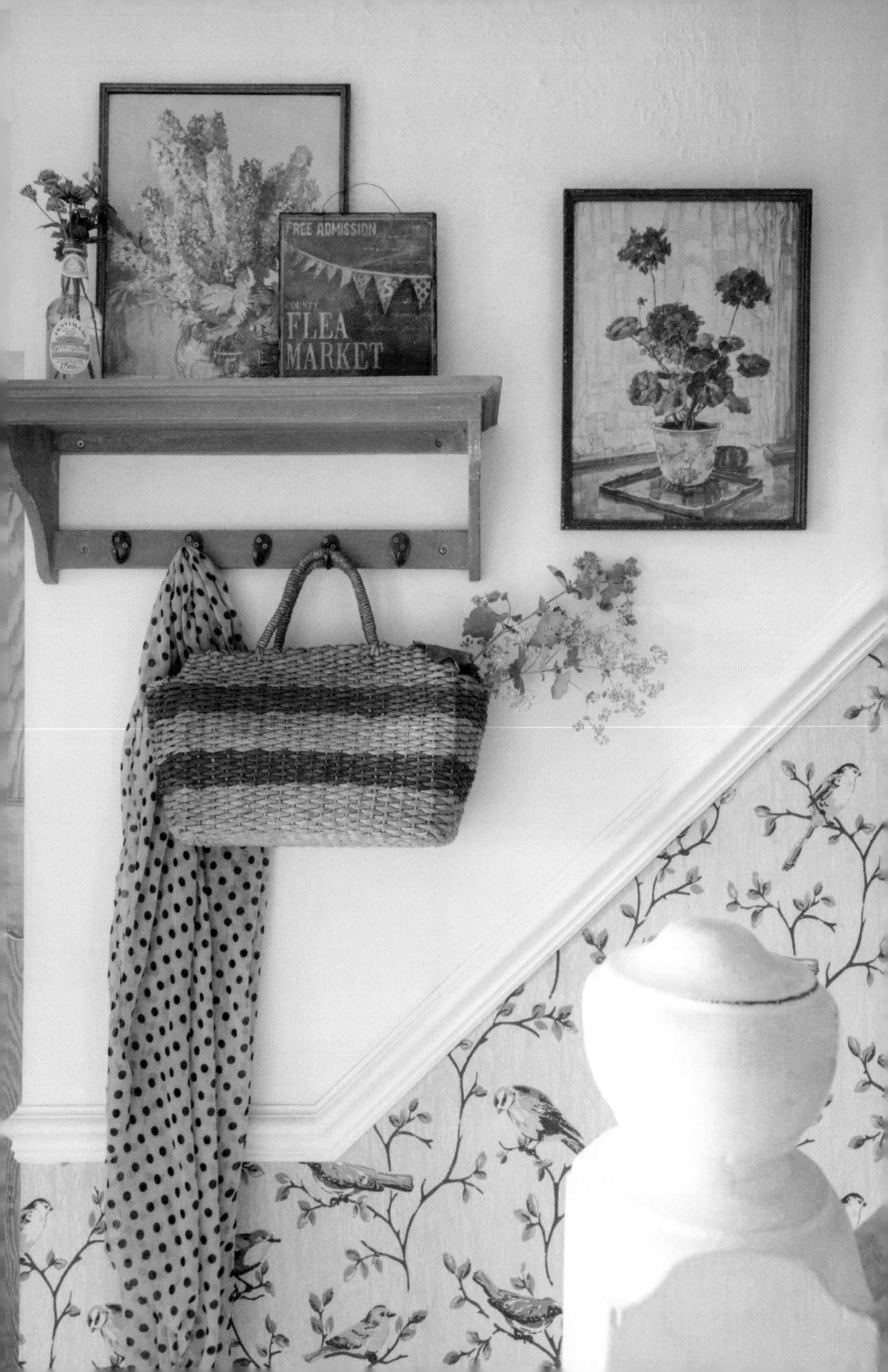
FREE ADMISSION
COUNTY
FLEA
MARKET

# Furnishings

The way you furnish your house is possibly the most powerful way you can affect its character. You can transform almost any style of home, built in any era, into a cottagecore haven, simply by selecting the right furniture and arranging it a certain way. For the cottage aesthetic, think practical, rustic furniture with history and charm, pieces that will stand the test of time and tell stories long after you have finished using them, and ones that welcome guests into your cozy, comfortable home. To create the ultimate cozy cottage atmosphere, textiles are also a must. Think soft throws, giant cushions, and thick, knitted blankets, or a warm, luxurious carpet beneath bare feet after a long day at work.

**Ideas to get you started:**
*Wooden, farmhouse-style pieces such as rocking chairs, scrubbed kitchen tables, and Welsh dressers; wicker baskets and trunks; writing bureaus and reading chairs; vintage couches, armchairs, and chaise longues; repurposed coffee tables and stools; mismatched kitchen chairs and wooden benches; grandfather clocks; log burners, open fires, range cookers, and bundles of firewood; needlework cushions, herringbone throws, eiderdowns, blankets, and bedspreads; natural, organic fabrics such as cotton, linen, silk, wool, and jute; sheepskin rugs; botanical-inspired patterns that reflect the changing seasons; oriental and Persian rugs; bedroom ceiling canopies and patchwork quilts; heavy curtains for winter, and light, organza drapes for summer.*

# Lighting

Appropriate lighting is an essential part of a healthy, happy home.
Among other things, it has been proven to reduce stress, as different
colors and levels of luminosity are known to influence our mood, even
if we don't realize it at the time. It has also been proven that feelings
of sadness and depression are more prevalent in places with less light.
When the right lighting is achieved, a room can be transformed. And
it's often one of the easiest and most affordable ways to refresh and
revamp your living space.

**Ideas to get you started:**
*Lanterns, oil burners, tealights, and scented candles; vintage
candlestick holders; the light of an open fire; fire pits and garden
bonfires for toasting marshmallows and making cocoa; strings of fairy
lights along the walls; large, clear windows to let in the sunlight; dim
evening lamps to wind down for the night.*

# Trinkets

Is there anything better than scouring thrift
stores and antique stores to find a new treasure to
take home? Whether you love collecting old paintings
or tiny sculptures of birds, there is a place for everything
beautiful in the world of cottagecore. If something sparks joy
for you, there is a place for it somewhere, and it's an art in itself
to arrange your treasures on the perfect shelf or mantelpiece.
Each item is a reflection of who you are and another simple
way you can express yourself through the personality
of your home.

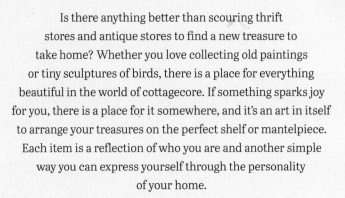

**Ideas to get you started:**
*Ornaments and ceramics; oil and watercolor paintings and
drawings, especially those created by friends and family or collected
in special places; book displays of old classics, best-loved stories,
and favorite covers; cuckoo clocks; old horseshoes; letter writing
sets, typewriters, quills and ink; vases, pots, and trinket dishes;
mismatched silverware and tableware; glass jugs and mason
jars; deep, sturdy mugs for tea, coffee, and cocoa; stove top
moka pots, percolators, and vintage French presses;
whistling stove top kettles; egg holders, toast
racks, and butter dishes.*

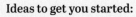

# Decoration

Similar to lighting, decorating your home is one of the most affordable ways to revamp the space and give it a new lease on life. It's also the perfect way to hone in on those cottagecore aesthetics, from chintzy printed wallpaper to matte-painted color schemes. You may want to cover everything in floral patterns, or you may want to keep it minimal with light grays and pastels. Whatever your style, take the opportunity to redecorate in your own way, making your cottage sanctuary extra comfortable and inspiring to be in. Think feature walls, mismatched botanical patterns, vases of cut flowers, and trailing houseplants in every corner.

**Ideas to get you started:**
*Earthy, pastel-toned color palettes in matte paint, especially white, cream, light gray, and natural colors; vintage wallpaper designs inspired by flowers, plants, and chintz prints; lots of houseplants, succulents, and vases of cut flowers scattered around the home; dried herbs and flowers hung from the ceiling.*

# Clean and green

"What better way to keep your home sparkling and fresh than by using planet-friendly concoctions that you can make in your own home?"

WITH MOST OF US BECOMING MORE AND MORE environmentally conscious, it is important we make the right decisions when choosing what we buy and use in our homes. Regular cleaning products may do the job well, but they can be damaging to the environment after they have disappeared down the drain, polluting ecosystems that are already fragile and under threat. There is now a huge range of eco-friendly cleaning products for sale in grocery stores and health stores, but they can be expensive and still heavy on plastic use. That's why the best solution is to make your own products! What better way to keep your home sparkling and fresh than by using planet-friendly concoctions that you can make in your own home? There's nothing more satisfying than being able to keep a clean, cozy home without causing harm to our precious planet. The following recipes are all made from simple, store cupboard ingredients; they're cheap and cheerful, and most importantly, they don't contain any of the harmful chemicals that can damage local ecosystems and human health. They will also save you plenty of money, as you can reuse and refill the containers, and buy ingredients in bulk to cut costs.

# All-purpose cleaner

A great all-rounder for wiping down surfaces around your home. The acidity of the vinegar helps dissolve grime, and although the vinegary smell should disappear as it dries, the essential oils will also help to offset it. Store away from sunlight, and use within a year for best results.

**You will need:**
*2 cups (480 ml) water*
*2 cups (480 ml) white vinegar*
*5 drops lemon oil*
*5 drops thyme oil*
*1 spray bottle*

1. Pour the water into a clean spray bottle.
2. Add the vinegar and essential oils, using more or fewer drops for a stronger or weaker scent.
3. Replace the spray top tightly, and shake well before use.

# Glass cleaner

A simple solution for sparkling windows, mirrors, and shower doors. Not only does the vinegar dissolve grime, but the fine granules of cornstarch act as a natural abrasive to remove stubborn marks. Store away from sunlight, and use within a year for best results.

**You will need:**
*¼ cup (60 ml) white vinegar*
*4 cups (960 ml) warm water*
*1 tablespoon cornstarch*
*10 drops peppermint oil*
*1 spray bottle*

1. Combine all the ingredients in a clean spray bottle.
2. Replace the spray top tightly, and shake well to diffuse the cornstarch.
3. Spray on glass and mirrors, and remove with a dry cloth or piece of newspaper.

# Toilet cleaner

Avoid pouring nasty chemicals into the water and try this natural alternative instead, perfect for leaving your toilet sparkling and ready to go. You can also experiment with your favorite essential oils if you want that "freshly cleaned" scent.

**You will need:**
*1 cup (240 ml) white vinegar*
*¼ cup (45 g) baking soda*
*10 drops peppermint oil*

1. Pour the vinegar around the bowl of the toilet, then sprinkle the baking soda over the top, followed by a few drops of peppermint oil.
2. Leave it to sit for 5 minutes, then scrub with the toilet brush, allowing them to fizz together and clean the bowl as they go.
3. Flush to rinse.

# Air freshener

This is a simple and effective way of clearing the air of everyday smells such as pet odors, cooking, and smoke. Experiment with your favorite essential oils—but remember to include the olive oil, too. This acts as a carrier, diluting the essential oils so that they don't cause irritation if they come into contact with your skin.

**You will need:**
*10 drops essential oil—try blending orange, lemon, and bergamot for an uplifting scent*
*4 teaspoons olive oil*
*1 spray bottle*

1.  Pour the essential oil and olive oil into the empty spray bottle and shake from side to side to mix.
2.  Carefully fill the spray bottle with fresh water, secure the lid, and give one final shake to combine.
3.  Spray through the air and over couches, armchairs, rugs, and cushions.

# Furniture polish

This natural polish will help protect wooden furniture, doors, window frames, and countertops. The olive oil nourishes and conditions wood, while the citric acid in the lemon juice gently lifts stains. As the lemon juice is fresh and won't last long, only make as much as you need in one use.

**You will need:**
*½ cup (120 ml) olive oil*
*¼ cup (60 ml) lemon juice*

1.  Pour the ingredients into a clean, open container, and stir with a spoon to combine.
2.  Dip the corner of a soft, dry cloth into the mixture and rub along the grain of the wood, repeating until the entire surface is covered.
3.  Remove any residue with another clean cloth.

# Carpet freshener

Sprinkle this over carpets, rugs, and floors to freshen up the home. This recipe works with any essential oil, but wild orange and cinnamon are known for their purifying and deodorizing properties. For best results, only make as much as you need in one use.

**You will need:**

*1 cup (180 g) baking soda*
*½ cup (50 g) cornstarch*
*5 drops wild orange oil*
*3 drops cinnamon oil*
*Sprinkling jar or sieve*

1. Combine the baking soda and cornstarch in a bowl, then add the essential oils and stir well.
2. Pour into a sprinkling jar or use a sieve to dust onto carpets as needed.
3. Wait for at least 30 minutes, then vacuum to remove the mixture.

# Mold & mildew spray

This simple recipe will help remove mold and mildew from damp areas. Open the windows wide while spraying to avoid the vinegar smell becoming too intense, but don't worry—it will disappear once dry. The tea tree oil is a natural fungicide, which is effective at killing mold spores.

**You will need:**

*10 drops tea tree oil*
*4 tablespoons olive oil*
*1 spray bottle filled with white vinegar*

1. In a container, mix together the tea tree oil and olive oil until combined. Add these to the spray bottle of vinegar, and shake well to mix.
2. Spritz over the affected area and leave for 30–45 minutes before rinsing off with warm water and a soft sponge—or a tougher cloth if the stains are stubborn.

# Bringing
# the outside in

"Human beings are nurturing by nature; we love
to form connections with other living things."

O UR LOVE OF HOUSEPLANTS HAS ALWAYS BEEN CELEBRATED IN
one form or another. The Victorians were so obsessed with
collecting exotic ferns, they gallivanted around the world in
search of the most dazzling species, a phenomenon that was even
given its own name: pteridomania (fern fever). Today, there has been
a huge resurgence in indoor plant ownership, particularly among
millennials connecting with other collectors via their colorful and
calming social media feeds. But keeping houseplants is more than
just a passing trend. Human beings are nurturing by nature; we love
to form connections with other living things, take care of them, and
invest emotionally in their wellbeing. Studies have proven a range
of psychological and physical health benefits associated with indoor
gardening, including improved mood, reduced stress levels, increased
productivity in office environments, improved attention span, reduced
blood pressure, and a decrease in fatigue and headaches. Other
advocates believe that tending to their plants gives them a greater
sense of fulfillment and purpose.

# Easy-to-grow houseplants

Whether you are looking to brighten up your living space, oxygenate the room, or simply connect with another living thing, get started on your indoor garden with this list of easy-to-grow houseplants.

## Useful tools

**Watering can**—aim for a sturdy, lightweight can with a long, narrow spout rather than a sprinkler.
**Mister**—perfect for tropical plants that enjoy humidity.
**Soil probe**—if you're not great at watering routines, a soil probe will tell you when a plant is thirsty.
**Pruning shears**—easy to maneuver into narrow spots for trimming and shaping.

**Lemon tree**
Bring the balmy vibes of the Mediterranean into your own home with a simple yet elegant lemon tree. The trees themselves are fairly easy to care for, but not everyone succeeds in growing an actual lemon. Soil must be kept moist and well-drained, but the most important things to consider are the light and temperature. Indoor lemon trees need close to eight hours of sunlight each day; the more light they are exposed to, the more likely you are to be squeezing fresh lemon juice onto your morning pancakes. They also grow best with nightly temperatures near 65°F (18°C), and away from air conditioning and heating ducts. For an extra boost of goodness, consider popping your lemon tree outside in the warmer summer months.

## Jade tree

This beautiful succulent, native to South Africa, requires plenty of sunlight and very little water, which is why it suits beginner plant lovers best. The soil must also be relatively nutrient poor, with no extra fertilizer added. Jade trees, also known as the "lucky plant" or "money tree", can also be trimmed and shaped like bonsai trees. Not only is bonsai a wonderful skill to learn in itself, it also teaches patience, creativity, and connection with nature—all values that are celebrated in the world of cottagecore.

## Rosemary

A fragrant, evergreen herb native to the Mediterranean region of Europe, rosemary grows easily in warm gardens, but will also survive indoors if given a little care. It's worth it though; the smell of rosemary is aromatic and cleanses the air, while the sprigs can be added to roasting dishes for extra flavor. Rosemary thrives with lots of light and careful watering, so be sure to grow it on your brightest windowsill, and keep it well hydrated but without waterlogging the soil.

## Boston fern

Ignite your inner pteridomaniac with this popular, blue-green plant, also known as the sword fern. Native to the swampy tropics, it is particularly fond of humid environments, so a bathroom full of indirect sunlight makes for the perfect spot; its bright green leaves will start turning yellow if the air is too dry. The Boston fern is thought to be one of the best plants for purifying the air, removing toxins, and neutralizing smoke. It looks particularly lovely in a hanging planter or on a stand, where the leaves can cascade over the sides.

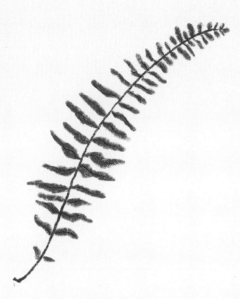

Chapter Four

# Slow fashion and beauty

THE ART OF COTTAGECORE IS NOT JUST PRETENDING WE LIVE IN the past, but rather taking the more romantic, inspiring pieces of the past and weaving them into our modern lives. The same goes for cottagecore fashion. Inspired by the natural fabrics, pinafore dresses, floral prints, and vintage accessories of the past, we can find treasures in the stories of yesterday and use them to create our own narratives today. One week we can be the strong-hearted heroine of a Brontë novel, the next we can be wandering through deep, dark forests, or tending to the animals on our own make-believe farm. We can mix and match vintage pieces with contemporary style, abandon gender norms, and dip into past times to express how we truly feel.

American sociology professor, Juliet Schor, once observed that, as a society, we have become both too materialistic and not materialistic enough. In other words, we consume too readily without stopping to consider the real value of that which we consume. Nothing demonstrates this more than the modern fashion industry, particularly the "fast fashion" phenomenon we have all grown accustomed to in the last few decades. As individuals, it is not our fault

that the mass production of clothing has led to environmental damage and the exploitation of labor, but it is our responsibility to rethink the way we shop. The root of the problem is that clothing is now made and sold too cheaply, although that doesn't necessarily mean we have to fork out hundreds of dollars on "ethical" brands, if we don't want to. So, what are the alternatives?

Like everything in the world of cottagecore, it's all about reimagining what we think of as normal. In turning away from fast fashion and slowing things down, we can reuse, recycle, borrow, and stitch our way to a more creative and compassionate wardrobe. The same goes for our beauty products, if we choose to use them. Having a more mindful approach means taking note of the ingredients we use, the brands we support, and even ditching some store-bought products altogether in favor of making our own natural remedies. In a world of convenience and quick spending, it has become an act of gentle rebellion to step back and consider our choices more carefully.

# Curating a cottagecore wardrobe

"Bring different fabrics into your everyday wardrobe, such as delicate floral and gingham prints."

WHEN CURATING A COTTAGECORE WARDROBE, DRESSES ARE one of the easiest places to start, as they come in so many sizes and shapes, and have been popular throughout history, in one form or another. Brands such as Laura Ashley and Liberty have championed floral prints and vintage-style dresses over the last few decades, which means that—fortunately for us—you don't have to go too far back in time to find something to wear. You could also start by bringing different fabrics into your everyday wardrobe, such as delicate floral and gingham prints, natural materials such as linen and organza, vintage accessories and brooches, or even a simple flower in your hair.

## Fabrics

Natural fabrics are always best when dressing the part, and when sourced ethically, they are also usually kinder to our skin and the planet. Organic cotton is readily available in clothes stores, but you could also seek out linen pieces for the summer as they are cool and comfortable. In the winter, cord, tweed, and wool are great options for building up layers and keeping warm.

## Accessories

Flower crowns, straw hats, and hair ribbons are simple ways to brighten up your look. You can also find modern and vintage jewelry pieces such as choker necklaces, drop earrings, pearl necklaces, lockets, and brooches, or even a pocket watch for a really distinctive look. Lace-up boots are perfect for winter, or try ankle boots with frilled socks for the lighter months. And one of the easiest accessories to pursue your cottagecore style? A simple straw basket, perfect for going to the market, filling with foraged berries, or carrying a book and a thermos of tea for a walk in the woods.

## Outfits

Regency-style dresses are perfect for the *Pride and Prejudice* aesthetic, complete with empire waistlines, small, puffed sleeves, pearl necklaces, and hair ribbons. Prairie dresses are comfortable and bring the *Little Women* vibe—they are usually made of light cotton or cord fabric, with high necklines, long sleeves, full skirts, and paired with tights and boots. Smock dresses have a more relaxed fit, often with Peter Pan collars, puffed sleeves, and microprint patterns, and pinafores are a great addition over the top of dresses or blouses to evoke the more historic, farmhouse style of a cottage dweller. Overalls are a practical addition to the cottagecore wardrobe, or a simple ruffled blouse and jeans can give a more mainstream look an Edwardian twist.

# Sustainability

"With every purchase we make (or don't make),
we are making a stand for sustainable fashion."

A FEW DECADES AGO, FASHION WOULD NOT HAVE BEEN THE FIRST thing people thought of when they considered social and environmental issues. Yet, thanks to the internet and social media, it has become clear how damaging the fashion industry can be if companies do not follow an ethical model. Most of us have heard of "fast fashion," meaning clothes that are made at cut-rate costs to the detriment of everyone along the supply chain, not to mention the environmental damage caused by so much demand for cheap clothes. Fortunately, however, the power to change it all is in our hands, as with every purchase we make (or don't make), we are making a stand for sustainable fashion. In the world of fashion, sustainability means working toward carbon-neutral clothing, made in an ethical way with a focus on equality, social justice, animal welfare, and ecological integrity. Sounds good? That's because it is! And contrary to popular belief, sustainability doesn't have to mean spending more money. It can simply mean buying less, buying better, and reusing what has already been produced. We all love having a fresh new wardrobe—but wouldn't it be better if it was planet friendly, too?

# Wear less, waste less

They say the most ethical way to consume is simply not to
buy anything at all, and the same logic can easily be applied
to clothing. The most planet-friendly way to refresh your
wardrobe isn't to focus on bringing in brand new items, but
to give new life to preloved ones. Check out these simple
ways to get started:

### Make do and mend

It has become commonplace
to throw away clothes when
they are damaged or well-
worn, but this throwaway
culture is a relatively new
phenomenon. Only a few
decades ago, clothing would
have been mended with a
needle and thread and given a
brand new lease on life. If you
don't fancy it yourself, there
are plenty of repair shops and
communities that you can
delegate the task to.

### Swap with friends

Share your favorites with
your closest friends and
organize a swap-shop dinner
party. Pop some bubbles,
rustle up a home-cooked
meal, and have a fun night
in with your best friends.
Just ask them to bring along
their unwanted clothes, and
see which of your group
might be able to give them
a new home. It's free, fun,
and you never know what
might turn up.

### Rental fashion

Clothing rental services
allow you to rent items—
from a single piece to an
entire wardrobe—for a few
weeks or months at a time.
Not only is this a great way
to refresh your wardrobe
without buying more clothes,
but its circular economy
model is also less demanding
on the planet.

# Thrift shopping

To buy secondhand is to curate a wardrobe full of stories, and to stumble upon a thrift store is to walk into a cave of wonders. Who wove this sweater by hand? Who got married in these ivory shoes? Where was this hat designed, and why did they choose this particular shade of rusty red? The magic is in the mystery, and in finding unique pieces and giving them a new life, we forge a connection with people we will probably never meet and spin our own stories in turn. Not only are we revaluing our clothes, we are also reducing our pressure on the planet and saving a few pennies as we go. What's not to love? Mildly disorganized and ever-changing, thrift stores can seem intimidating to beginners—but once you become familiar with their ways, you'll never look at new clothes in the same way. To start, think about the best places in your local area to visit; more affluent towns and districts are more likely to have higher-quality donations and might be worth an extra bus ride. Give yourself plenty of time to slow down and rummage through, and remember to be open minded.

### Vintage handbags

There are plenty of people who would rather give their designer bags away than bother selling them, so keep an eye out in your local thrift store to see if any goodies turn up. The genuine article may even come with a certificate of authentication to prove that it's real, but otherwise look closely at the quality of the stitching, lining colors, and material.

### Upcycled beads

A box of costume jewelry is a feast for the eyes in any thrift store. Not everything will be to your taste, but how about picking and choosing your favorite pieces and rethreading them to make something brand new? You could take the brightest, boldest beads and put together a statement necklace for a friend, or even have a go at stringing together your own earrings.

### Old band tees

Is your best friend a die-hard heavy metal fan? Or perhaps your father-in-law just can't get enough of '80s synth rock? Thrift stores are full of old band tees from long-forgotten gigs, which make the perfect gift for loved ones who have a passion for their music. Keep an eye out in the men's and women's T-shirt sections to see what pops up.

# Upcycling

Have you ever spotted a piece of clothing in a thrift store and loved the print, but weren't sure of the shape? Or loved the color, if only it were in your size? That's the mystery of thrift shopping—there are no multiple sizes for everyone, only unique pieces of treasure waiting for the right home. The good thing is, however, that you can take a thrift store treasure and make it your own through the art of upcycling. Whether it's clothing, furniture, or something else altogether, upcycling simply means to reuse and refurbish an item in such a way that it becomes more valuable than when you bought it in the first place. A ripped, baggy old shirt might look like it's only good for rags, but with a little mending and some carefully placed embroidery, you could upcycle it into something wearable. Stuck for ideas? Check out these basic ways to upcycle an old garment:

### Potato block printing

Remember printing with potato blocks as a child? Don't be fooled by the simplicity of this craft. Potatoes are an easily accessible way to get started with block printing, allowing you to transform a plain piece of fabric by adding your own beautiful hand-carved prints. All you need is some basic fabric paint and a little patience, and you could upcycle anything from T-shirts to tote bags, leggings to laptop cases.

### Sewing and scissors

Nothing beats the old-fashioned art of stitching and mending. Got a hole in your favorite T-shirt? It's amazing how easy it is to mend something with a needle and thread. Take a look at page 38 for an easy guide to darning. You can also sew on patches and patchworks to upcycle your old clothes, or use scissors to chop and change one thing into another. How about cropping a pair of jeans or turning a T-shirt into a tank top?

### Plant-based fabric dyes

Did you know you can use plants—and even vegetable peelings—to dye your clothes? From turmeric and avocado skins to beets, carrot tops, elderberries, and onion skins, once you've mastered the basic technique of plant-based dyeing, there are endless ways to experiment. It's best to use light, natural fabrics, and make sure you buy a mordant, a type of fixative that will help bind the dye to your fabric and help it survive the washing process.

# Natural cosmetics

"Sometimes the simplest ideas
are the best."

T HE COSMETICS INDUSTRY IS A COMPLICATED ONE. READ THE back of a product label and you're guaranteed to find a big list of ingredients you have either never heard of, or you're not exactly sure what it is they do. Few of us can claim we know exactly which of these ingredients are good for our skin, our bodies, or the world around us. And while there are plenty of ethical brands now leading the way in terms of transparent and eco-friendly ingredients, these can still come with a hefty price tag. So, why not try making your own cosmetics instead? Sometimes the simplest ideas are the best, and you often don't need anything fancier than the natural ingredients already given to us by Mother Earth. Try out these simple ideas and see what works for you.

# Apple cider vinegar hair rinse

Ever heard of a hair rinse? It's not quite shampoo, not quite conditioner, but works a little like both to give you beautiful, shining hair and a healthy scalp. Apple cider vinegar is a bit of a wonder product when it comes to natural beauty. Proponents claim it can improve shine, increase volume, combat dandruff, reduce itchiness, balance pH levels, exfoliate the scalp, aid growth, and deep clean your hair. Avoid using it if you have very dry hair; colored hair should use the rinse once a week at most; and if you have an oily scalp and hair, once or twice a week is perfect.

**You will need:**

*½ cup (100 ml) apple cider vinegar*
*2 cups (500 ml) fresh water*
*24-ounce (700 ml) glass spray bottle*

1. Pour the vinegar and water into the spray bottle, and stir well to combine.
2. Spray the mixture over the top of your scalp generously so it is evenly coated.
3. Use your fingers to gently massage the mixture into your hair, then let it sit for 3–5 minutes before rinsing it all away with cool water.
4. Follow the rinse with a light conditioner, then rinse with water until your hair is squeaky clean.

# Sea salt spray

Looking for those effortlessly tousled, sea-sprayed locks you see on all your favorite Instagram feeds? This recipe is a simple and inexpensive solution. To prevent the salt drying out your hair, it contains aloe vera and jojoba oil, which will both help condition your hair and keep it shiny. Try spritzing it over damp or dry hair and then scrunching into loose curls, or for more dramatic waves, try spraying it onto damp braided hair before bed and unraveling in the morning.

**You will need:**
½ cup (120 ml) water
1 tablespoon sea salt
1 tablespoon aloe vera juice
½ teaspoon jojoba oil
4-ounce (125 ml) glass spray bottle

1. Heat the water to a gentle boil, then remove from the heat and add the sea salt to the pan, stirring until dissolved.
2. Allow the mixture to completely cool. Then, add the aloe vera juice and jojoba oil, stirring well to combine.
3. Once everything is mixed, pour into the spray bottle and store in a cool, dry place when not in use.

# Peppermint foot soak

The antibacterial and antifungal properties of peppermint make this a powerful and soothing way to relax and revive tired feet. The olive or coconut oil also helps to moisturize and replenish dry skin. You can store any excess mixture in a tub or bottle ready for use next time, as the sugar and oil will keep fresh for a few weeks at least.

**You will need:**
1 cup (200 g) granulated sugar
3 tablespoons olive or coconut oil
20 drops peppermint oil

1. Place the sugar into a medium-sized bowl. In a separate container, gently combine the olive or coconut oil with the peppermint oil, then add to the sugar. Use your hands to stir the mixture until you have a grainy, sludgy consistency.
2. When it's ready, scrub the mixture over your feet to give an allover exfoliation, then place your feet in a large bowl of hot water (adjust temperature as required) to allow the scrub to fall away and transform into a soothing soak.
3. Leave feet to soak for at least 10 minutes, or until the water becomes too cold.

# Green tea face mist

Freshen up with a little bottle of face mist—
perfect for cooling you down, lifting you
up, and reviving your mood throughout the
day. Both green tea and tea tree oil have
powerful anti-inflammatory and antibacterial
properties, making this a great face mist for
oily or acne-prone skin.

**You will need:**

*1 teabag of green tea*
*½ cup (120 ml) hot water*
*2 teaspoons almond oil*
*4 drops tea tree oil*
*4-ounce (125 ml) glass spray bottle*

1.  Pop the teabag into the hot water and
    allow it to steep for 5 minutes. Remove
    the bag, and leave the tea to cool down.
2.  Meanwhile, put the almond oil and tea
    tree oil into the glass bottle, and shake
    gently to combine.
3.  When the tea has cooled, pour into the
    bottle, replace the top, and shake to
    combine. Remember to shake gently
    before each use.

# Turmeric face mask

Both honey and turmeric are powerhouses when it comes to skincare. Honey is anti-inflammatory and antimicrobial, while turmeric is loaded with antioxidants that are thought to help treat acne, brighten dark spots, and reduce fine lines. This warm, rich, easy-to-make face mask is a perfect treat for an indulgent night in.

**You will need:**

*1 tablespoon honey*
*½ teaspoon turmeric powder*
*10 drops kefir*
*1 tablespoon almond oil*

1.  Combine the honey and turmeric powder carefully in a bowl before adding in the drops of kefir. These will help prevent the turmeric from staining your skin—although if it does, don't panic. It won't be there long!
2.  Pop in the almond oil for an extra boost of soothing hydration, and stir it all together gently with a spoon.
3.  Once it's ready, apply a thin layer of the mask to clean, dry skin. Let it sit for 10–20 minutes before rinsing off with warm water, patting dry, and finishing your skincare routine as usual.

# Coffee bean face scrub

If you drink your morning coffee fresh from the bean, you probably find yourself scooping your used grounds into the compost without another thought. But did you know they can be recycled to make an all-natural face scrub? This recipe makes a perfect once-a-week scrub for exfoliating dead skin, improving circulation, brightening your complexion, reducing puffiness, and soothing redness.

**You will need:**

2 tablespoons used coffee grounds
2 tablespoons cocoa powder
3 tablespoons whole milk
1 tablespoon honey

1.  In a bowl, combine the coffee grounds and cocoa powder, stirring well to mix together.
2.  Mix in the milk until it starts to form a paste, then add the honey to stir into a smooth, creamy consistency.
3.  Apply to damp skin, using your fingers to gently massage it into the skin and buff away dead cells.
4.  Leave for 10 minutes, then rinse off with warm water and pat dry.

# Lip butter balm

The skin on your lips is thinner than anywhere else on your body, which is why it needs extra love and care. To keep your lips soft and supple, pop the balm into a small pot or jar, and keep it in your bag at all times to make sure you never go without. When sourcing the ingredients, make sure to buy cosmetic-grade quality, and opt for organic, if you can.

**You will need:**

1 tablespoon shea butter
1 tablespoon beeswax, grated or in pellets
1 tablespoon coconut oil
1 teaspoon honey

1.  Pop a pan of water on to boil, and place a heatproof bowl inside it, without letting the water enter the bowl.
2.  Add the shea butter, beeswax, and coconut oil to the bowl, and gently heat until melted together. Then add the honey, and whisk together to combine.
3.  Turn off the heat and allow to cool slightly, before pouring into your container of choice—the best option is a heatproof glass pot with a screw-on lid.
4.  Leave to cool fully before adding the lid.

# Chapter Five

# Grow
# your own

I T WAS VIRGINIA WOOLF WHO FIRST OBSERVED THAT: "ONE CANNOT think well, love well, sleep well, if one has not dined well." Is there any greater joy than a plate of fresh, home-cooked food? We are inundated with choices for our food in the modern day, but cottagers would have historically lived off the food in their own back garden, valuing simple, modest produce, and using their skills with herbs and spices to cook up something delicious. One of the joys of slowing down and living more closely aligned with nature is being able to connect with the seasons and notice which foods they produce, which fruits are ripening in the hedgerow, and which vegetables are emerging from the earth. On a rainy afternoon, there is nothing more calming than hunkering down at the kitchen table and preparing something tasty with your own hands, to enjoy yourself or share with loved ones.

We are also living in a world where people are increasingly keen to know where their food has come from. Cheap products with unfamiliar labels are all very well, but many now rightly insist on understanding the background of their food, particularly in terms

of animal welfare, environmental costs, and unethical ingredients. The world of cottagecore invites conversation surrounding what we consume and how we consume it, particularly as we try our best to care for the world around us. From eating seasonally to reducing waste, growing your own produce to home cooking, there are plenty of simple, rewarding ways to eat more mindfully, ethically, and beautifully. After all, what greater pleasure can there be than the taste of good food?

Even if we are short on money, time, or space, preparing and enjoying food can still be a relaxing and meditative part of our day. Whether it's stirring up a batch of overnight oats to eat the next morning, or preparing a sumptuous feast for friends on a rainy weekend, there are lots of ways to slow down and nurture a more mindful relationship with our food. And the more we embrace homemade, seasonal, local produce, the more we stop and notice the world around us, and the richer life becomes.

# Eating seasonally

"When we eat in-season produce, it is fresher,
perfectly ripe, and tastes better and sweeter."

I T IS DIFFICULT TO IMAGINE, BUT TRAVEL BACK A CENTURY OR TWO
and our dinner plates looked very different to how they do
now. We were much more closely connected to the food in the
ground, rarely importing anything, and instead living on what our
local farmers grew for us, or what we grew ourselves. Fast forward
to the twenty-first century, and our grocery stores are full of bright
and beautiful fruits and vegetables from all around the world. It is
wonderful to have access to so many interesting and healthy foods, but
the consequence is that we have lost touch with our seasonal rhythms.
When we eat in-season produce, it is fresher, perfectly ripe, and tastes
better and sweeter. These foods will have been naturally ripened on
the vine or in the earth and harvested at exactly the right time, giving
them more flavor and nutritional value. Eating seasonally is not only
good for our own wellbeing, it is much more affordable due to the
supply meeting the demand and plays an important role in looking
after the planet.

# Seasonal produce

Depending on where you live in the world, your seasonal
produce will look different, but here's a good starter list to find
out what's available to eat right now within the US:

## Winter

The season for root vegetables buried deep in
the ground, as well as dark, leafy greens and
zesty citrus fruits, perfect for a midwinter
vitamin boost.

*Broccoli, brussels sprouts, cabbage,
cauliflower, grapefruit, kale, leeks, lemons,
mushrooms, onions, oranges, papayas,
parsnips, pears, pomegranates, rutabagas,
sweet potatoes, tangelos, tangerines, turnips.*

## Spring

The earth begins to stir and the world wakes
up; look for tart spring flavors and fresh salad
leaves unfurling into the warm sun.

*Apricots, artichokes, asparagus, broccoli,
brussels sprouts, cauliflower, cherries, leeks,
lettuce, mangoes, mushrooms, okra, parsnips,
pineapples, radishes, rhubarb, rutabagas,
spring peas, strawberries, Swiss chard,
turnips, zucchini.*

## Summer

Indulge in sweet, summer fruits and juicy
vegetables ripened by the summer heat—
perfect for picnics and alfresco dining into
the long evenings.

*Acorn squash, apples, apricots, blackberries,
blueberries, butternut squash, cantaloupe,
cherries, corn, cucumbers, eggplant, figs,
green beans, kiwi, kohlrabi, lettuce, mangoes,
okra, peaches, peppers, plums, raspberries,
strawberries, summer squash, Swiss chard,
tomatoes, watermelon, zucchini.*

## Fall

The golden hour for heavy, rich fruits fresh
from the hedgerow, as well as delicious root
vegetables to see you through the darkening
days ahead.

*Acorn squash, apples, beets, broccoli,
brussels sprouts, butternut squash, cabbage,
cantaloupe, cauliflower, cranberries,
eggplant, figs, grapes, green beans, leeks,
lettuce, mangoes, mushrooms, okra,
oranges, parsnips, peppers, persimmons,
pomegranates, pumpkins, rutabagas, spinach,
sweet potatoes, Swiss chard, tangerines,
tomatoes, turnips, winter squash.*

# Reducing food waste

"If we all play our part and think about
our food more mindfully, it's amazing what
a difference we can make."

DID YOU KNOW THAT AROUND A THIRD OF THE FOOD WE PRODUCE and buy globally goes to waste? Whether it's spoiled crops on the ground, lost stock in transit, imperfect products left on the grocery store shelf, or the food that we throw away at home, it's a huge problem that we can all help to tackle. Not only is food waste terrible in itself, it is also a waste of money and resources, and puts additional pressure on the environment in lots of different ways, including waste disposal, intensive farming, and excess water use. It has become one of the most damaging elements of our modern agricultural system, particularly as food is now so cheap, but fortunately there is also a lot we can do to prevent food waste in our local communities and our own homes. All it takes is a little care and thought, being more selective with the food we buy, and thinking more seriously about how we will prepare and eat it. If we all play our part and think about our food more mindfully, it's amazing what a difference we can make.

# Making better choices

The best way to make your weekly shop more ethical is to buy less and make the most of what you already have. We are all tempted by the glitz and glamour of grocery store deals, but do we really need everything that is advertised? There are better, more compassionate ways to shop without breaking the bank, starting with the fundamental question: what do we really need?

**Buy only what you need**
If you regularly end up with too much food in the fridge, or ingredients you have no idea how to use, try planning your meals before you shop. Make a list and stick to it, avoid impulse buys, and buy only the amounts you and your family will need.

**Choose the ugly ones**
Oddly shaped and bruised fruits and vegetables are often thrown away because they aren't visually perfect, despite being entirely edible and just as tasty as their comrades. Try choosing the ugliest products on the shelf, and reduce the chance of them being thrown away later.

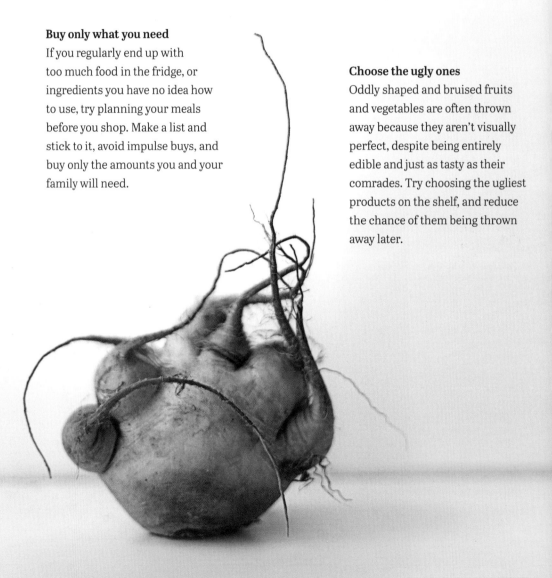

**Use every inch**
We often throw away parts of our fruits and vegetables without realizing they are edible too. For example, did you know you can eat the leaves of beets, cauliflower, and broccoli? Kale stems, apple skins, asparagus ends—even if something isn't as sweet or succulent, it can often still be used in other ways. When in doubt, boil everything up to make a vegetable stock that you can freeze and use at a later date.

# Using leftovers

Food waste is one of the most pressing issues in the modern world, but as individuals, there is plenty we can do to help combat it, starting with the fruits and vegetables in our own kitchen. You'll be surprised how rewarding it feels to reduce how much you throw away, and you'll probably save a few cents along the way too. You might even learn a few new tips and tricks for using up old ingredients. Here are a few simple things that we can all do to make the most of our food:

### Sharing is caring

There are now loads of apps, websites, and social media groups that can connect people looking to reduce their food waste. These can put locals in touch with each other to share surplus food, alert you to unwanted food from businesses nearby, or guide you to places that need unwanted food donations. Get connected and learn more about your local community.

### Love your leftovers

It can be difficult to guess the right portion size sometimes, so if you end up with a crock pot full of leftovers, just pop them in the fridge and eat them for lunch the next day. You can also freeze and reheat them later, or even use them in a different meal entirely, such as hash browns or mixed vegetable soup. It's a great way to save money and time!

### Compost, compost, compost!

Almost all your food scraps are suitable for the compost heap, which is the perfect way to give nutrients back to the soil and reduce your carbon footprint. If you don't have outdoor space and the local authority doesn't collect kitchen waste, see if a neighbor, local community garden, or gardening group might be interested.

# Growing your own

"The love that goes into carefully growing your own
food brings rewards far beyond the ones on your plate."

NOTHING BEATS THE FRESH FLAVORS OF FRUITS, VEGETABLES, AND
herbs grown by hand in your own garden or outdoor space.
It's one of the most satisfying achievements, and also makes
it far easier to live a slower, healthier, and more sustainable lifestyle.
Gardening is an incredibly mindful and nurturing hobby, and the
love that goes into carefully growing your own food brings rewards
far beyond the ones on your plate. From drizzling fresh rain water
onto tiny green shoots, to harvesting your goods at the end of the
season, there is nothing more nourishing for both the soul and
stomach than to tend to your own cottage garden and grow your
own plate of delicious, seasonal food. Even if just one of the items
on your plate is produced by hand, that little morsel will taste all the
better for the love you poured into growing it. Start small, and see
where your green fingers take you!

# Getting started

You don't need a large space to begin growing—a well-lit window box is enough to get started with a simple kitchen herb garden. Try these tips for setting up your own fruit and vegetable patch:

## Choices

Begin by writing down your favorite fruits, vegetables, and herbs, then use a little research to cross off those that won't grow easily in your native climate. You can then think about the space you have available for growing, and remove any that won't be suitable. For example, if you only have space for a small raised bed in the garden, you might like to start with just one or two vegetables, such as zucchini and onions.

## Timing

Make a list of the sowing and harvesting times of everything you would like to grow, and work backward from there. You will usually find this information on the back of seed packets, or, if you want to speed the process up slightly, you can also buy young plants instead of seeds. The benefit of these is that they are germinated by professionals and are more likely to survive into maturity, although they are slightly more expensive.

## Space

Use the packet information to work out how far apart to space your crops, as some will produce a huge harvest while others will be more sparse. If you have the space, making rows of lots of different crops will mean you always have something ready to harvest. If you're working with a small space, such as a tiny patio or a window box, there are plenty of options available, including dwarf varieties that have been specifically bred to thrive in small spaces. Make use of vertical space with climbing plants and hanging baskets.

## Community gardens

Remember, if you simply don't have the space at home, there are other options! Most towns and districts have private and publicly owned community gardens available to hire, in which locals can dedicate the space to growing whatever produce they fancy. These are also wonderful places to meet fellow growers, share tips, swap excess produce, and make friends.

# Foraging

"Foraging was a vital part
of daily life for our ancestors."

THE ART OF FORAGING IS ALMOST AS ANCIENT AS HUMAN civilization itself. One of the first adaptations made by our species was the transition to hunter-gatherer status, as we taught ourselves to hunt wild animals and gather plants to sustain ourselves. In a world before online shopping and takeout pizza, foraging was a vital part of daily life for our ancestors, and one on which they depended to stay alive. And although, today, we may rely more on grocery stores, there is still a place for foraging wild food in the modern world. When carried out sustainably and respectfully, foraging is an incredibly environmentally friendly choice, as there is no reliance on chemicals and pesticides, the food is seasonal, and there is no carbon footprint from importing and transportation. Your food can literally be harvested fresh from the ground and carried lovingly to your own kitchen table, ready to be savored and devoured. Imagine scooping a thick blob of blackberry jam onto a piece of warm toast and dreaming of misty woodland walks and fall skies, or biting down on the earthy crunch of hazelnuts fresh from the husk, or tasting the salt crystals hidden in a frond of seaweed.

# Starting with the basics

If you're new to foraging, start with the basics. Nettles, dandelions, blackberries, wild garlic, and elderflower are all easy to identify, fairly abundant, and simple to prepare and cook. Use the seasons to guide you—look out for fresh greens and flowers in spring and summer, fruits and nuts in the fall, and mushrooms in winter. Edible greens are great to start with—common species across North America include wild lettuce, mallow, sweet fennel, plantain, purslane, lamb's-quarters, and chickweed. Later in the year, look for vitamin-rich fruits such as raspberries, blueberries, cloudberries, cranberries, bilberries, currants, lingonberries, bearberries, and crowberries, all of which can be stewed into a sweet pie.

The best thing about foraging is the thrill of finding a new species, but remember the golden rule: if you're not 100 percent sure, don't pick it. There are plenty of additional resources online that can help you feel more confident with identification, and social media is a fantastic place to ask others for help.

Remember, a good forager is an ethical one. Pick only the amounts you need to ensure plant populations remain healthy, and leave plenty for the birds and other wildlife. Remember to keep to public places, as it is illegal to trespass or forage on private land without permission.

Foraging is a great way to spend more time in nature and connect with the world around us. Not only does it encourage us to learn about different species of trees, shrubs, seaweeds, herbs, nuts, fruits, seeds, and mushrooms, it also helps us engage with the landscape as a whole. When we keep a closer eye on the natural world, we are more likely to notice other animals, birds, and insects, protect their habitats, and appreciate the fragility and complexity of our ecosystems.

You don't need expensive equipment, but it is always worth dressing for the weather and perhaps bringing a thermos of tea, Tupperware tubs, scissors, and gardening gloves. If you're still unsure where to start, there are plenty of foraging clubs around in which beginners and experienced foragers can meet and learn together.

## Elder

Taking its name from the Anglo-Saxon word *aeld*, meaning "flame," the stems of the elder were said to be hollow and used as a natural bellows to aerate the fire. Early in the summer, the boughs are strewn with sprigs of frothy, lime-cream blossom, which then ripen into clusters of dark elderberries. Although not great to eat raw, the berries can be used to make wine, cordial, fruit crumble, syrup, jam, chutney, or spiced buns, and can also be added to homemade mead—a mixture of honey and water left to ferment in a demijohn —where they bring a sweet earthiness to the flavor. Look out for them growing around rabbit warrens, as the rabbits gobble up the berries and distribute the seeds in their droppings.

## Nettle

Delicious, healthy, and a little bit stingy, nettles are a common plant that taste best in the spring. Cook young leaves and shoots like spinach, sautéing in butter, garlic, and salt for extra flavor, or add the leaves to hot soups, sauces, and stews. Nettles make an excellent home-brewed beer, and when left to settle will produce a clear, russet draft with a wonderful, wild tang.

## Dandelion

An underrated plant, the dandelion can be found all over the world and grows all year round. Try to collect the flower heads early in the morning to ensure the freshest flavor; these have a delicate taste and can be used to make dandelion wine. Young flower buds can also be pickled like capers and young leaves can be eaten raw in salads or cooked like spinach. The root can also be cooked in the same way as parsnips and eaten as a side vegetable, or roasted and ground to make an intriguing coffee substitute.

## Blackberry

One of the first fall berries to arrive is the glossy, purple fruit of the bramble shrub. They first grow green and then red, before turning a dark purple when ready to eat. Snack on them raw from the twig, or use them in pies, jams, syrups, and wine.

# Slow kitchen projects

"The slower the process,
the more meditative it becomes."

ONCE YOU'VE GROWN OR FORAGED A FEW TREATS, WHAT HAPPENS next? Cooking and baking are great ways to transform simple ingredients into something delicious for the kitchen table. Working with food can be incredibly mindful and help you escape the chaos of the outside world. The slower the process, the more meditative it becomes and the more rewarding it feels to taste the final product. Making your own food is also generally much healthier than buying it prepackaged, especially when so much food is ultraprocessed and full of ingredients that don't need to be there. One of the most relaxing ways to spend a few hours at home is to potter about the kitchen, washing vegetables, simmering jam, or kneading bread ready for the oven. It's a wonderful way of reconnecting with your hands, as well as learning to appreciate the work and energy that goes into our food, which is often taken for granted. Try these four slow kitchen projects to help you reconnect with the process and appreciate a quieter pace in this noisy world.

# Baking bread

Nothing smells more delicious than a loaf of freshly baked bread, but part of the joy comes from the process it takes to get there. Unlike a sponge cake or a batch of cookies, the art of breadmaking takes several slow, precious hours. First you mix the ingredients, then knead by hand—a process that many find meditative and cathartic—then you allow the bread to proof, knead again, proof again, and finally it is ready to bake. Make a mistake somewhere along the line—whether it's rushing the kneading or finishing the proofing too early—and the loaf will turn out slightly askew. Breadmaking is the ultimate exercise in patience, physical effort, and attention to detail, but it's all worth it for that fresh, warm slice covered in salted butter. For an additional challenge—and extra reward—you could also try sourdough bread, which requires you to nurture a "living" yeast starter.

# Jams & jellies

Got a glut of windfall apples in the fall or a basket full of blackberries with nowhere to go? The best way to use up your tastiest fruits is to pop them in a jam or jelly, preserving them for months to come and rewarding your future self with a pot of sweet, oozing stickiness to smother on toast. The difference between jam and jelly is simply that jam contains the whole fruits, whereas jelly contains the strained juices without the flesh. Jam is perfect for using up apples, pears, blackberries, and anything else that you can eat every part of. Jelly is good for fruits with stones or pips that are difficult to sieve out, such as plums, damsons, sloes, and rose hips. All you need is a pot, a stove, some clean jars, and an afternoon to dream away over a simmering pan of gooey fruit. And, if you end up with too many jars for yourself, they make great holiday gifts for friends and family.

# Home brewing

The process of brewing beer, mead, cider, and wine on a small scale is fun and experimental. The opportunities are endless—from fizzing elderflower champagne and dark nettle beer, to the sweet honey mead favored by the Vikings. The method for brewing alcoholic drinks is a fairly simple one, and you only need a few pieces of equipment to get started. These include a large pot and bucket, a demijohn and airlock, a siphon tube, bottles, and caps. You will also need a little permanent storage space in which to keep your bottles brewing, as they take time to develop. One of the easiest ways to start is with honey mead, as you only need the basic ingredients of honey and water. You could also try buying a home brewing kit with all the ingredients and equipment ready to go, as this will take you through each step with plenty of guidance.

# Fermentation

Fermentation is the name given to the process that breaks down carbohydrates through the use of bacteria and yeast. It gives food a distinctive, but not unpleasant, tartness and is used to make common foods such as yogurt, cheese, and alcohol. More recently, studies have shown that eating some kinds of fermented food can have a positive impact on gut health and wellbeing, as it promotes the growth of beneficial bacteria known as probiotics. It is easy to get started with fermenting your own foods at home, and the process is as slow and satisfying as the rest. All you need is patience and a few jars and pots, and perhaps the willingness to try some new flavors! To get started, you could experiment with making your own sauerkraut (fermented cabbage), kefir (fermented yogurt), sourdough bread, kombucha (fermented tea), or kimchi (fermented cabbage and radish).

# Chapter Six

# Embracing nature

I MMERSING OURSELVES IN THE NATURAL WORLD CAN BE ONE OF
the strongest antidotes to the chaos of modern life. As a society,
many of us have become disconnected from the natural world, but
there is nothing like stepping out into the woods or heading down to
the shore, listening to the rhythms of nature washing over us as we
breathe fresh air and feel the wind in our hair. Whether the sun is
shining or it's pouring with rain, being outdoors is the ultimate feel-
good sensation, even if it's just for five minutes at the end of a busy day.

This "nature cure" has been scientifically proven to reduce stress,
improve physical health, and increase feelings of wellbeing. Our
world can be one of anxiety, overwork, and digital overwhelm, where
a moment of peace or solitude seems difficult to come by. Our lives
are busy ones, and it can often feel impossible to stop and breathe,
to take the time to pause and reflect inward. When we feel anxiety

descending, as so many of us do, we can head out into our local green spaces to watch birds soaring overhead and bumblebees dancing over the wildflowers. Often, the simple touch of tree bark or the crunch of leaves underfoot is enough to reset a busy mind.

Nature is restorative, no matter the season, and nurturing a connection with the outdoors is not only good for us, but also for the world around us. When we observe the comings and goings of other species, we form an emotional connection and begin to care more about their wellbeing, both as individuals and on a larger scale. So get outdoors, fill your lungs with fresh air, and feel the warm sun on your skin. Experience nature in all its glory, and you will begin to feel the benefits of more time spent outdoors. We are only animals after all, and animals are born to live under open skies.

# The dawn chorus

"While we snooze in our own nests, we are missing
out on the greatest wake-up call on earth."

THE WARM DAYS OF SPRING AND SUMMER OFFER SO MUCH JOY
each year, and the dawn chorus in particular is one of nature's
most powerful and captivating spectacles. From four o'clock
onwards our gardens, woods, and forests erupt into a cacophony
of song as every male bird attempts to seduce a partner with the
greatest operatic aria of their lives. For most of us, the dawn chorus is
something to stumble upon by accident; a sleepless night, newborn
baby, or all-night party might lead us to a surprise performance, but
by the time most of us wake up, the chorus has faded to the simple
tweets and chirrups that we hear over our first cup of coffee. Could it
be that while we snooze in our own nests, we are missing out on the
greatest wake-up call on earth? An energy boost more powerful than
any yoga class or double-shot macchiato—a burst of inspiration from
the lungs of nature itself? Research has shown that exposure to nature
can reduce the risk of hypertension, cardiovascular illness, anxiety,
depression, and fatigue, as well as improve our life satisfaction, vitality,
happiness, and mindfulness. Could it be that rising with the sun and
listening to the awakening natural world might improve our wellbeing,
even if just once or twice a week? Treat yourself to an early night, open
the window wide, and wake up to the sweet, melting reverberations of
birdsong at dawn. The joy will linger in your bones and carry you all
the way through to sunset.

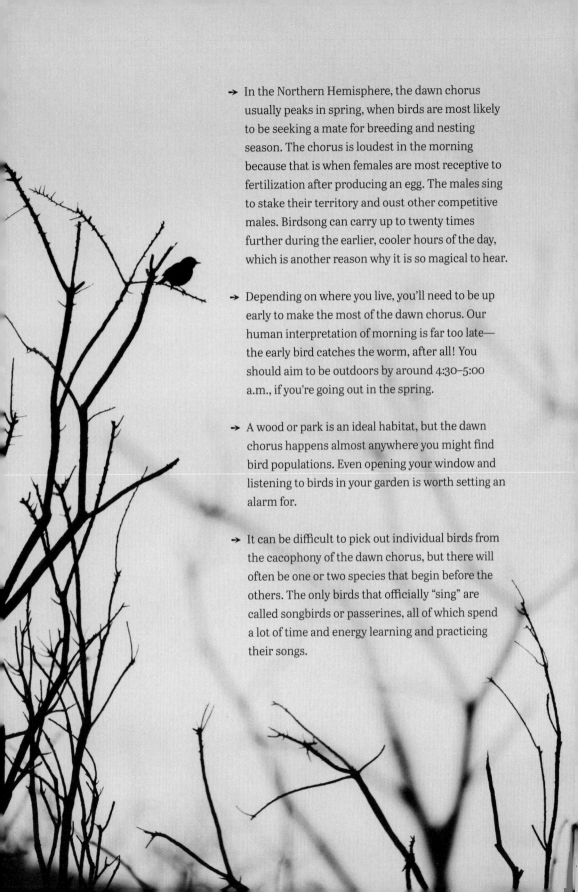

→ In the Northern Hemisphere, the dawn chorus usually peaks in spring, when birds are most likely to be seeking a mate for breeding and nesting season. The chorus is loudest in the morning because that is when females are most receptive to fertilization after producing an egg. The males sing to stake their territory and oust other competitive males. Birdsong can carry up to twenty times further during the earlier, cooler hours of the day, which is another reason why it is so magical to hear.

→ Depending on where you live, you'll need to be up early to make the most of the dawn chorus. Our human interpretation of morning is far too late— the early bird catches the worm, after all! You should aim to be outdoors by around 4:30–5:00 a.m., if you're going out in the spring.

→ A wood or park is an ideal habitat, but the dawn chorus happens almost anywhere you might find bird populations. Even opening your window and listening to birds in your garden is worth setting an alarm for.

→ It can be difficult to pick out individual birds from the cacophony of the dawn chorus, but there will often be one or two species that begin before the others. The only birds that officially "sing" are called songbirds or passerines, all of which spend a lot of time and energy learning and practicing their songs.

# Wild swimming

"Time spent in nature is never wasted."

I N THE CHAOS OF MODERN LIFE, THERE IS NOTHING SO RESTORATIVE
as finding a stretch of quiet water and immersing yourself in
it. You can forget the bright lights and rushed schedules of
ordinary working days; for a while, you can escape into a forgotten
world, imagining life centuries ago when time passed slowly, survival
was hard, but humans were deeply connected with nature and the
landscapes around us. Time spent in nature is never wasted, and
within the flowing water of a river we can feel the sun on our skin and
fresh air in our lungs, as we drift sleepily away into another world.
The sea, too, can be a wonderful source of rejuvenation. The waves
push down on the shore in an endless rhythm, arriving and departing,
embracing and withdrawing. There is nothing so magical as running
to meet the water as it sweeps up and crashes down, being carried
back to the sand like driftwood. Trying to stand against the tide or
swim upriver is like trying to stop time; better to float through it,
uncontrolled, and embrace the rhythm of the water.

# Dipping your toe in

Wild swimming has grown in popularity over the last few years, but there are a few important things to consider when taking the plunge. Wherever and whenever you choose to take a dip, be sure to use your common sense and avoid venturing beyond your comfort zone.

→ The magic of outdoor swimming is the chance to feel connected to nature, with the cold, fresh water swirling around you, birds in the trees, and the sun on your skin. But there are measures to consider when you leave the safe, chlorinated confines of the swimming pool and head out into the wild. Be sure to check the depth of the water, as well as any currents or tides that could overpower you or carry you away. Keep an eye on the temperature too; if the water is too cold, consider wearing a wet suit.

→ It's always best to avoid swimming alone. Take a friend or family member on your wild adventure, or join an outdoor swimming group to make new friends and enjoy the water together. If swimming with a friend isn't possible, you could invest in a tow float that can give you something to hang onto, as well as being bright and colorful to attract attention from passersby.

→ Water pollution is an important factor to consider when choosing a swimming spot. Unfortunately, many of our waterways are polluted by the illegal discharge of waste material, industrial spoils, sewage spills, and the overuse of fertilizers and agricultural chemicals. This can make some bodies of water dangerous to swim in, so always check before you go to make sure your wild dip is safe and healthy.

→ Before entering the water, always make sure you know how you will get out. Warm up with some light exercise before and afterward, and try to wear footwear if you can. Some busy rivers can have other forms of pollution such as broken glass and rusty metal, so do protect your feet, even if it's just by wearing a pair of flip-flops.

# Kit list

While there's nothing to stop you leaping into the water for a spontaneous swim, sometimes it's better to plan things out. Consider using the following items to make your new hobby more comfortable:

**Swimsuit**—for milder temperatures, a normal swimsuit will probably be fine. For colder climates, or for those who aren't used to cold-water swimming, a wet suit will take the edge off the cold.

**Goggles**—if you'd like to dip your head below the surface and explore the underwater wilderness, goggles can be useful.

**Swimming cap**—a brightly colored cap will not only keep your head warm, but it also signals to other river users that you are in the water.

**Whistle**—a light addition to any swim, giving you an extra option to call for help if you get stuck or come into trouble.

**Towel**—a big, dry towel will be a welcome sight when you leave the cold water. You might also enjoy a thermos of something hot such as tea or coffee and a few cookies—the perfect way to warm up on the shore!

# Stargazing

"Gazing at the night sky can make our daily problems and worries feel insignificant."

THE NIGHT SKY HAS IGNITED OUR IMAGINATIONS FOR THOUSANDS of years, which is perhaps why the late cosmologist Stephen Hawking advised us to "look up at the stars and not down at our feet." All around the world, communities have woven stories into the patterns they've found in the stars, from hunters and beasts to wrathful gods and goddesses. Through science and careful observation, we have learned to understand the night sky and our place within it, but up until the last century it still remained just out of reach—a sea of lights beyond the veil of our atmosphere. Then, in 1969, three men became the first to land on another celestial body and walk on the surface of the earth's moon, 238,855 miles (384,400 km) away from where humans sat watching on their black-and-white television sets. It is considered to be one of the most remarkable achievements in our species' history, but the sequence of events that got us there started with one thing: stargazing. In our anthropocentric, pressurized world, gazing at the night sky can make our daily problems and worries feel insignificant. At the same time, it's a reminder that a precise cluster of atoms came together to form our exact minds and bodies, living beings on a living earth. When the Voyager 1 space probe took the famous *Pale Blue Dot* photograph in 1990, we saw our planet for what it really was—a single pixel against the vastness of outer space. If nothing else, looking up at the night sky reminds us how precious our planet is and how important it is to protect our only home.

# Getting started

Stargazing is a simple pleasure—all you need is a relatively dark sky and your own eyes to enjoy it. But, if you want to make the most of a night beneath the stars, there are a few additional things you might want to consider.

→ The most important piece of stargazing equipment is your eyes, adapted for night vision. It can take your eyes up to 30 minutes to fully adjust to the dark, especially if you have recently been exposed to bright lights. So, the first thing to do is find a spot that's as far away from light pollution as possible.

→ One thing to remember is the moon, which can act as another source of light pollution and drown out the details of the fainter stars of the Milky Way. It's important to check the phases of the moon, as the closer you can get to a new moon, the better the conditions for stargazing.

→ There are lots of useful books that can show you the constellation lines and give you more information about the stars within them. You can also use an app—most have a feature that allows you to point your phone at the sky to identify the constellations you're looking at. However, be aware that if you are using your phone while stargazing, you may lose your night-adapted vision, so try to lower the brightness of your screen or find an app that uses night mode to turn your display dark.

→ If you want to take a closer look, you might want to invest in a pair of binoculars or a telescope. Binoculars are a great place to start to practice navigating the night sky, especially if you require something portable or don't have the space for a telescope. As well as deep sky objects, such as galaxies or star clusters, they are also fantastic for looking at planets and the moon. Telescopes are a more powerful but less affordable option, but you could get in touch with your local astronomy group to try one out.

→ Be sure to keep warm, as outdoor spaces are often much colder than people expect, even during summer. Wear thermals and plenty of layers, and taking a big thermos of something warm is never a bad idea either. You'll be grateful for it if you are heading out on a cold night!

# Gazing throughout the year

For most people around the world, stargazing is a year-round hobby that can be enjoyed throughout the seasons. But you can get to know the night sky even better by keeping an eye on the calendar to see what's making an appearance each month. These are the best night sky objects and constellations to see in the northern hemisphere:

## January

Ursa Major: *the great she-bear constellation contains the Big Dipper group of stars and is visible all year round; in winter and early spring, it lies close to the horizon.*

Quadrantids: *this is one of the most active meteor showers with up to one hundred meteors seen per hour, appearing to radiate from the constellation Boötes.*

## February

Orion: *the mythical hunter constellation whose star-studded belt straddles the celestial equator; from the northern hemisphere, look to the southwest.*

Venus: *known as the "evening star," look for this bright planet in the western sky just after dusk.*

## March

Cassiopeia: *a W-shaped constellation named after the vain queen from Greek mythology; look high up in the northwest sky.*

Moon: *the spring equinox marks the date when the day and night are of equal length; the full moon that waxes around this date is known as the last moon of winter.*

## April

Leo: *one of the largest constellations in the sky; look for the brightest star Regulus just after nightfall.*

Lyrids: *this meteor shower radiates from the constellation Lyra; it is best seen between midnight and dawn.*

## May

Boötes: *the herdsman constellation containing Arcturus, one of the brightest stars in the night sky; he can be seen driving his great plow, or Big Dipper, in a circle around the North Star.*

Eta Aquarids: *a meteor shower radiating from the constellation Aquarius, with up to thirty meteors visible per hour.*

## June

Lyra: *locate this harp constellation by finding Vega, the second brightest star in the night sky; look to the northeast after dusk.*

Moon: *in the Northern Hemisphere, the summer solstice occurs when the North Pole is tilted closest to the sun; the full moon that waxes around this date falls around the shortest night of the year.*

## July

Scorpius: *a constellation containing the bright star Antares, known as the "rival of Mars" because it appears to shine red; Scorpius lies low along the southern horizon.*

## August

Saturn: *look low in the southeastern sky, and to the naked eye Saturn might be mistaken for a star; you will need a telescope to see its rings.*

Perseids: *this meteor shower has historically recorded up to one hundred meteors per hour; find them from midnight to dawn, radiating from the constellation Perseus.*

## September

Jupiter: *use binoculars to see this planet, shining like a silvery star; a telescope will reveal its famous Great Red Spot.*

Moon: *the fall equinox marks the date when the day and night are of equal length; the full moon that waxes around this date is known as the last moon of summer.*

## October

Pegasus: *the most distinctive feature of the flying horse constellation is its "Great Square," made up of four bright stars; look to the eastern sky.*

Draconids: *this minor meteor shower peaks in the early evening, just after sunset; it radiates from the serpentine constellation Draco.*

## November

Andromeda: *a constellation in the eastern sky containing the Andromeda Galaxy, the most distant object visible to the naked eye.*

## December

Taurus: *just northwest of Orion, the bull constellation lies between Aries and Gemini.*

Geminids: *a shower of bold, white meteors that radiate quickly from the constellation Gemini; most visible between midnight and dawn.*

Solstice moon: *in the Northern Hemisphere, the winter solstice occurs when the North Pole is tilted furthest from the sun; the full moon that waxes around this date falls around the longest night of the year.*

# Botanical drawing

> "Drawing is another way we can connect deeper with the world around us."

WHEN WAS THE LAST TIME YOU PICKED UP A PENCIL AND sketchbook? For many of us, it may not have been since our school days, convinced we weren't "good enough" at drawing, leading us to seek other pursuits instead. But the truth is that anyone can draw, and the art of observation that develops with drawing is another way we can connect deeper with the world around us, especially when it comes to nature and landscapes. Learning to observe the way a flower opens in spring, how an apple rots in the fall, or even studying the feathers on a magpie in the garden are all special ways we can interact with nature and capture what we see in pen, ink, or paint. It doesn't matter what your final piece of art looks like, only that you spent time connecting with nature and the pencil in your hand. If you want to track your progress, you could keep a nature journal to document your sketches through the seasons. But don't allow pressure to put you off—the most important thing is to experiment and have fun without worrying about the end result.

# Getting started

Humans have been drawing pictures for thousands of years, so don't worry about getting it right straight away. Enjoy the process by getting back to basics and simply embracing the sensation of pencil moving over paper and creating something new. Find somewhere comfortable to sit, gather up your favorite pencils, and see which plants and flowers you are drawn to most. It could be the smallest weed or the most ostentatious flower—all are beautiful in their own unique way.

→ Try not to focus on creating lifelike drawings if you don't find it enjoyable. Embrace the style of art you love, whether that's wobbly, organic designs or something completely abstract. The most important thing is observation and how your brain translates what it sees onto the blank page.

→ Take the time to learn about the plants and flowers you are drawing. Not only will it help you appreciate their form and improve your work, but it will help you nurture a deeper connection with the natural world as a whole.

→ Cut flowers are easy to transport, but they wilt and fade more quickly than plants left in the ground. Pop them in a vase of fresh water to extend their life. Potted plants retain their natural form, even when moved around.

→ Establish a focal point from which you can start your drawing, then examine each of the shapes, junctions, and textures that emerge from that point. It's tempting to start with an outline of the whole subject, but that doesn't always lead to a satisfying piece of work.

→ If pens and pencils aren't your medium of choice, switch to watercolor or acrylic paints, or branch into linocut printing, chalk, or charcoal. Drawing is a great foundation skill to develop, but there is no need to make botanical art a chore.

→ Try not to compare your work to other people's, unless you are looking for tips to capture difficult parts of the plant. Your work is beautiful because it's unique—don't worry about what anyone else's looks like!

→ Practice, practice, practice. The best way to develop your work is to embrace the mistakes, learn from the process, and keep pushing forward. It's amazing how quickly your skills will improve!

# Chapter Seven

Pen and paper

T HE KETTLE HAS BOILED, A CANDLE GLOWS ON THE KITCHEN
table, and you are about to settle down for an evening of
solitude with only a pen and paper for company. Sound
dreamy? In our technology-focused world, we have all understandably
become a little too dependent on our phones and computers, so to
spend quality time with something that doesn't emit blue light has
almost become a luxury. There is something about the gentle scratch
of the pen, the rustle of paper as you flick through a notebook or turn
over a new leaf, that is both calming and inspiring. There is even a
special beauty in the mistakes and crossings out, marks of the writer
that haven't been erased by the click of a keyboard button.

There's a reason we still value the quiet joy and power of pen
and paper. Creative writing has been proven to bring a whole host of
emotional benefits, while journaling is a great way to process thoughts
and declutter our brains. We can also use letter writing to simplify our

relationship with others, ditching the emojis and hashtags in favor of real, longform communication with friends and loved ones. When was the last time you wrote a letter to a friend instead of sending a casual text? When we dedicate time to pen and paper, we are giving more of ourselves to the conversation and rebelling against the quick, throwaway process that our modern communications have become.

There is power in the art of writing; we can project our voices around the world if we wish, all from the comfort of our own kitchen table. We can send our thoughts across land and sea, write postcards, send clippings and photographs, even nurture romances with loved ones far away. Whether we are writing a poem about the beauty of the leaves in fall, or telling our local political representative what we think of their approach to climate change, there is nothing we can't achieve using the gentle power of the written word.

# Journaling

> "Indulge in some much-needed self-care time, and see which thoughts spill out of your pen and onto the page."

A S CHILDREN, MANY OF US WILL HAVE BEEN FAMILIAR WITH THE concept of a secret diary. A place to share our most private thoughts, sort through our shifting emotions, and find a few moments of clarity—complete with a cheap padlock we were *certain* nobody could break through. The padlock may have disappeared, but keeping a diary or journal is still just as important for our adult minds as it was back then. Keeping a journal is a form of private therapy, proven to help reduce stress, improve immune function, keep our memory sharp, boost our mood, and strengthen our emotional functions. Whether we're just recording the events and emotions of the day, or writing a novel's worth of words every night, there is no right or wrong way to keep a journal. It doesn't matter if you have five minutes to spare or two hours—just grab a cup of tea or coffee, indulge in some much-needed self-care time, and see which thoughts spill out of your pen and onto the page. Don't worry about investing in an expensive notebook if you don't want to—a simple, spiral-bound one from the dollar store will do just fine, along with a cheap pen or pencil. Magic!

# Getting started

Journaling is all about giving yourself the time and space to explore
your own thoughts. There is no wrong way to journal; the most
important things are to find a way to fit it into your schedule and keep
it enjoyable. Try not to set yourself unrealistic expectations, but enjoy
making time for yourself and see where the pen and paper take you.
Remember—this is a simple, flexible, and accessible form of self-care.
You deserve to take a few minutes for yourself when you can.

**Building habits**

➔ Don't get bogged down
with being consistent or
motivated all the time.
Like all habits, journaling
can take a while to work
into your regular routine,
and there's nothing worse
than feeling guilty if you
don't manage to pick up a
pen every day. We all lead
busy lives, so do what you
can, and once you start
seeing the benefits it'll be
easier to keep it going.

**Start small**

➔ If a blank page is too
intimidating, start small.
Write a single line of
thought, an emotion
of the day, or even
something mundane
like what you had for
breakfast. It all helps to
move your brain cogs into
the right gear.

**Freewriting**

➔ Another effective
journaling technique
is freewriting. The idea
is to sit down every day
and fill three pages in
your notebook without
worrying about the
words you're actually
writing. This stream-of-
consciousness style is
said to help clear creative
blocks and remove the
pressure of writing
perfect prose every time.
Instead, you can simply
declutter your brain of
thoughts in the hope
that it might reveal
something new.

# Journaling prompts

Not sure where to begin on your journaling journey? Start with these writing prompts. They're a great way to trigger new ideas and get your pen flowing over the paper. Recognize how the prompts make you feel, allow yourself to explore those thoughts, and go forward from there.

→ Reflect on your life so far and explore what draws you to the cottager's life. What are you seeking, and how do you think you might find it?

→ In Roman mythology, Janus was the two-faced god of beginnings and endings, doorways and passages. What lessons from the past can you take forward into the future? And which elements would you like to let go of?

→ They say time can heal the deepest wounds and help us see things in ways we couldn't before. What do you know to be true now that you didn't know a year ago?

→ How do you feel today, and how do you *want* to feel today? Gently explore why there might be a difference between the two. How can they be more aligned in future?

# Writing letters

"By slowing down and focusing on the task, you might discover there's more on your mind than you ever imagined."

WHILE THE INTERNET AND SOCIAL MEDIA HAVE revolutionized the way we communicate, sometimes it can be healthy to step back from the digital world and return to a more mindful way of staying in touch. The next time you're looking to catch up with an old friend, embrace the power of snail mail and write them a letter. The simple joy of choosing the paper, opening your favorite ink pen, and scratching a handwritten message to a loved one has stood the test of time and will continue to do so, no matter how much further technology advances. By slowing down and focusing on the task, you might discover there's more on your mind than you ever imagined.

Have you ever felt powerless in the face of current affairs? We see so many issues in the news every day, but as individuals it can sometimes feel like there is little we can do to effect change. This, however, is not true. Throughout history, individuals have made huge differences to their local communities and countries as a whole, and it often begins with something as simple as a letter. The pen, as they say, is mightier than the sword, and it's amazing what can be achieved through communication alone. If you feel passionate about the world around you, from environmental issues to homelessness, never be afraid to write a letter. Whether it's a letter to your local political representative, the CEO of a business, a public figure you admire, or even the president themself—you never know how powerful your words might be. Just remember to be polite and express your views clearly, and who knows? You could well receive a letter in return and start driving real, positive change.

# Great letter writers

Looking for literary inspiration? Dive into the words of some of the greatest letter writers of all time. Their writing perfectly captures the time period they lived in, their own thoughts and emotions, and the beauty that exists within a simple conversation between friends.

### Jane Austen's Letters

(Oxford University Press, 2011)

*If Austen's six full-length novels have left you wanting more of her wit, wisdom, and keen observation, this volume of letters will illuminate her world.*

### George Orwell: A Life in Letters

(Liveright, 2013)

*A witty, personal collection of letters that tell stories from Orwell's life, share conversations with other political and artistic figures, and reveal why he chose his pen name.*

### Letters of Emily Dickinson

(Everyman, 2011)

*A beautiful collection of whimsical, humorous, and deeply moving letters to family and friends, written by one of the best-loved American poets of the nineteenth century.*

### Selected Letters of Virginia Woolf

(Vintage, 2008)

*Beyond her novels and short stories, Woolf's letters give us one of the finest views of the life of the British intelligentsia in the first half of the twentieth century.*

### The Letters of Vincent Van Gogh

(Penguin, 1997)

*An enigmatic figure to all who knew him, Van Gogh's letters give a little more insight into one of the most creative but haunted minds in the history of art.*

# Creative writing

> "There is no limit to what you can produce with the humble pen and paper."

THE BEAUTY OF CREATIVE WRITING IS HOW INFINITELY VARIED IT can be. From poetry and songwriting to novels, plays, scripts, short stories, blogs, journalism, zines, and podcasts, there is no limit to what you can produce with the humble pen and paper, or word processor. Studies have shown just how beneficial creative writing is for our wellbeing, whether it's building confidence in ourselves and enabling self-expression, boosting our imaginations, clarifying our thoughts, improving our linguistic skills, encouraging empathy and communication, or even improving our mental and emotional health. Writing has even been proven to alleviate stress levels and ward off intrusive, anxious thoughts. But you don't have to be a professional to reap the rewards of a creative-writing practice. Nurturing a simple writing habit, no matter how much you write or who ends up reading it, is a great way to get in touch with your creativity and dust off the corners of your mind you may have forgotten about.

# Writing poetry

Poetry is one of the easiest ways to let loose with your pen, simply because there are so many forms it can take. Whether you love rhyming sonnets, haikus, or sprawling free verse, have fun with the written word, and don't worry about sticking to the rules.

### Read lots of poetry

As with all creative practices, the best way to start forming your own ideas is to find inspiration in the work of others. Not only is reading poetry an enjoyable hobby, it will fuel your subconscious and get your own mind whirring into action.

### Start small

Don't worry about writing epic, page-long poems if you're new to the practice. Start by playing around with short-form poems such as the haiku, or, if you love rhyming poems, you could start by writing a limerick.

### Begin anywhere

Don't worry about the first line if it's not coming to you organically. Start by scribbling all your ideas down on the page and worry about their placement later. You'll be surprised at how quickly your poem will form itself.

### Embrace the thesaurus and dictionary

There's no shame in using tools like these to expand your vocabulary and help you shape your lines. We can't know all the words all the time!

### If you're stuck for an idea, try telling a story with your poem

Edgar Allan Poe was great at this, as his famous poem "The Raven" demonstrates. Poems don't have to be about abstract concepts—they can simply be a fun, rhythmic way to tell a story.

### Follow your passions

Poets, just like other artists, all communicate about different subjects. Some write about political topics, social injustice, climate change, and gender equality, while others prefer to write simply about the flowers in their garden or the moon in the sky. All subjects are valid—the most important thing is to be authentic to yourself and write what you feel truly passionate about, so try not to compare your work to others'.

# Other forms of creative writing

Caught the writing bug? It might be time to find different ways to express yourself. Sharing your work is a great way to develop your style, gain an audience, and engage with other creatives. If you don't feel ready to share yet, you could write under a pseudonym. Try these different forms of creative writing and see which one inspires you the most.

### Write a blog

Blogging might sound a little 2012, but it is still a brilliant and valuable way to share your work, develop your style, and allow others to engage with what you do, all from the comfort of your home and with little to no cost. Simply choose a subject to write about, sign up for a free account on any number of blogging platforms, hit publish—and you're away. Sharing on social media will also draw new readers in.

### Write a podcast

Almost everyone seems to have their own podcast these days, and that's because it's one of the best ways to communicate with the world. You don't need to spend a huge amount to get started either. The best podcasts start with a USB microphone, a well-designed logo, and great ideas transformed into brilliant audio content. Your writing skills can be used to script a podcast on any number of ideas, the more niche the better. Have fun and get your voice heard!

### Write for your local newspaper

Passionate about the people and places around your local community? Get in touch with your district's newspaper or magazine and offer your skills. You might want to write a monthly nature column, report on live events, or interview people of interest. You'd be surprised how often editors are looking for new voices with fresh ideas, so never be afraid to offer and see where the conversation takes you.

### Enter competitions

It's never too early to start entering work you're proud of into local, national, and even global competitions. Everybody starts somewhere, and some of the most prestigious writers in the world caught their lucky break by submitting their work to a contest. Most have small entry fees, but many are free to enter. You have nothing to lose by giving it a go, and you never know where it might lead.

# How to make a zine

Zines (a shortened form of "magazine" or "fanzine") are self-published, printed works that are typically produced in small, limited batches. They were first popularized during the mid-twentieth century, when science fiction writers used them to share their stories. Today, they are still an inexpensive and creative way for an artist to share their work, from poetry collections and graphic stories to linocut prints and political statements. If you're keen to share your work with a wider audience, making a zine might be the answer, and thanks to online marketplaces like Etsy, it's easier than ever to get your work into new hands.

### STEP 1: **Inspiration and research**

First, pick a theme for your zine. It could simply be a volume of your latest poems, or you might have themed a new collection of drawings around a current event or political issue. Give your zine a name, choose the size and page length, and start piecing together your ideas around this theme.

### STEP 2: **Writing and illustration**

Gather together the primary material for your zine, and then decide whether you want to fill any of the remaining space with anything else. For example, you may have written a collection of three short stories—do you want to illustrate them with line drawings or photographs? If you're not comfortable branching into a different creative skill, you could reach out to others you know to see if they'd like to collaborate. You'll also need to think about designing a front cover.

### STEP 3: **Composition**

The last step before sending everything to print is to arrange it on the computer. Or, if you're going down the more traditional route, you could arrange everything physically and use a photocopier to reproduce it. If working on a computer, make sure any images are scanned in, cropped, and edited, and the contents and end pages are all in the right place. You don't need any expensive software for this—there are plenty of free programs that will do the job.

### STEP 4: **Printing and distribution**

After everything has been arranged, it can all be exported as a PDF and sent to print. There are lots of online companies that specialize in producing zines, or you can just print them as booklets or pamphlets. Alternatively, you can produce them at home on your own printer—the beauty of the zine is in its rustic simplicity. If you print as a limited edition, remember to number each copy on the back. Once you're finished and happy with the final product, you can pop them online to sell, give them out as gifts to friends, or share them at craft fairs and markets.

# Creative writing prompts

Prompts are a great way to get your brain whirring and ideas flowing, especially when it comes to creative writing. They can take any form: you could flick through a newspaper, skim through the pages of your favorite book, or even jot down ideas from the radio. Simply use the prompt to generate new ideas, and see what happens when you put pen to paper. Take a look at the list below for some prompts to get you started:

→ You are a space tourist traveling alone to the International Space Station, which will keep you away from home for three years. You are looking back at the "pale blue dot" of planet Earth and decide to write a letter. Who is it for, and what does it say?

→ Three famous acquaintances have joined you round the table for supper. Who are they and what happens?

→ A blackbird takes shelter in your garden over winter. Each day it brings a piece of gold and leaves it as a gift on the window frame. What do you do?

→ Naturalists once believed that when migratory birds disappeared in fall, they were hibernating at the bottom of muddy ponds. Imagine you are one of these naturalists, and write a speech designed to convince your peers of your theory.

→ Imagine climbing a pine tree in midwinter. What can you see, smell, hear, and taste? What species do you find? What do you discover at the top?

→ You hear a magic flute while walking in the forest and decide to follow the sound. Where does it lead you? How does the journey make you feel?

# A cottagecore reading list

There's nothing more inspiring than settling down with a good book. From the windswept moors of England to the mountains of Middle Earth, begin your escape into the world of cottagecore with these essential titles. Who knows where the words and stories might take you?

*Anne of Green Gables*
by L. M. Montgomery

*Wuthering Heights*
by Emily Brontë

*The Wind in the Willows*
by Kenneth Grahame

*The Secret Garden*
by Frances Hodgson Burnett

*Little Women*
by Louisa May Alcott

*Heidi*
by Johanna Spyri

*The Hobbit*
by J. R. R. Tolkien

*Far from the Madding Crowd*
by Thomas Hardy

*Sense and Sensibility*
by Jane Austen

*Alice's Adventures in Wonderland*
by Lewis Carroll

*I Capture the Castle*
by Dodie Smith

*The Tale of Peter Rabbit*
by Beatrix Potter

*Howl's Moving Castle*
by Diana Wynne Jones

*The Tea Dragon Society*
by Katie O'Neill

*The Complete Brambly Hedge*
by Jill Barklem

*Wild Beauty*
by Anna-Marie McLemore

*Ella Enchanted*
by Gail Carson Levine

*The House in the Cerulean Sea*
by TJ Klune

*Sisters of Shadow*
by Katherine Livesey

*As You Like It*
by William Shakespeare

*Howards End*
by E. M. Forster

*Little House on the Prairie*
by Laura Ingalls Wilder

*Black Beauty*
by Anna Sewell

*Stardust*
by Neil Gaiman

*A Wizard of Earthsea*
by Ursula K. Le Guin

*Dracula*
by Bram Stoker

*Cranford*
by Elizabeth Cleghorn Gaskell

*Gulliver's Travels*
by Jonathan Swift

# Chapter Eight

# Getting serious

D REAMING OF LONG AFTERNOONS IN THE GARDEN, CANDLELIT, seasonal suppers, and cozy nights with a book? There is something incredibly tempting about the slow lifestyle advocated by the cottagecore trend, and if you've been inspired by the ideas explored in this book, a cottager's life might be for you. You don't need acres of land to live the cottagecore dream, but if you do have some extra space and a little time to try something new, there are plenty of hobbies, crafts, and pastimes that can transform you into a fully fledged cottager. Whether it's raising chickens or keeping bees, taking the next step in the cottager's lifestyle could enrich your life even further.

The following ideas require more time and commitment than the others explored in this book, but if you're tempted to try something new, I invite you to research the next steps and see whether these skills and crafts can help you to slow the pace of life, connect more deeply with nature, nurture your creativity, and learn more about the world around you. Even if you are short on space, there are lots of creative ways you can work around your limits, such as renting an allotment, sharing land with a friend, borrowing your parents' garden, or even converting an old outbuilding.

There are lots of resources online to help fuel your cottagecore vision, such as social media accounts, blogs, and entire communities founded on a shared love for an imagined rural paradise. The beauty of the internet is finding like-minded people who share all kinds of interests, no matter how niche! So, if you would like to share your cottagecore journey with others, or simply make new friends who understand your love for all things slow and beautiful, take a look online and connect with new people around the world.

On the other hand, you might like to keep your new lifestyle more private and offline. If you like, you could share it in person with friends and family members, join local community groups linked to your new hobbies, or even start your own cottagecore circle—complete with plenty of tea and cake! You could also start a cottagecore book club, textile group, gardening club, or craft group. Share your vision with friends old and new, and see where a collaborative approach might take you.

# Beekeeping

"Enjoy the satisfaction of providing
a safe home for bees."

IS THERE ANYTHING AS SATISFYING AS EATING WARM TOAST smothered with honey made by your own bees? Beekeeping is not only a rewarding and fascinating hobby, but when pursued ethically, it can really make a difference to local honeybee populations. You can produce your own honey and beeswax, either for yourself or for others, and at the same time you can provide a home for local honeybees who are already struggling with habitat loss around the world. If you prefer, you don't even need to harvest honey at all—you can just enjoy the satisfaction of providing a safe home for the bees.

The first step is to find your local beekeeping branch or community group, who will be able to get you started with everything you need to know. Once you've connected with other beekeepers, you'll want to attend a course to teach you all the basics. This will help you work out the best place to keep your hive, what equipment you'll need, how much money you'll need to invest, how much spare time is required throughout the year, and how to obtain your first swarm of bees. You don't need a lot of land to keep bees, but you will need an outdoor space for them to live and a few inexpensive bits and pieces to get started:

→ **Hive:** *the home for your swarm of bees.*

→ **Frames:** *these hold the foundation sheets in place, on which the bees will build honeycomb.*

→ **Beekeeping suit:** *to protect you from stings while caring for your bees.*

→ **Gloves:** *to help you handle the hive and frames.*

→ **Smoker:** *this calms the bees if you need to disturb the hive in any way.*

→ **Hive tool:** *a multipurpose handheld tool used to maintain and inspect the hive.*

# Chickens

"Keeping chickens is almost every cottage dweller's dream."

CHICKENS ARE FAIRLY EASY TO LOOK AFTER, MAKE WONDERFUL and characterful pets, and best of all—you'll probably have a constant supply of fresh eggs straight from your own back garden. Although chickens don't require too much maintenance, the most important questions to consider are whether you have the time every day to feed and check on them, whether somebody can be around to look after them when you're away, whether you can provide them with safe, predator-proof housing, and whether your outdoor space is secure enough to stop them going too free-range!

The chicken house or coop is the most important investment when considering chickens. This needs to provide suitable shelter in all weather and keep out predators. Beyond the house, they'll also need an enclosure in which to stretch their legs and socialize, plus a fresh supply of food and water. As for the chickens themselves, there are plenty of choices, including a range of pure breeds in all shapes and colors. You could also give a home to an ex-battery hen, some of which have rarely seen daylight in the intensive farming industry. Most of these will still give you plenty of eggs; they may not be as pretty as their pedigree counterparts, but they'll be very grateful for the second chance at life. Keeping chickens is almost every cottage dweller's dream. You will need these basics to get started:

→ **Chicken house or coop:** *to provide shelter and protect against predators.*

→ **Food and water:** *including kitchen scraps such as vegetable peelings.*

→ **Basket:** *for collecting eggs!*

→ **Coop cleaning tools:** *such as rubber gloves, brush, mop, bucket, dustpan, old cloths.*

→ **Medicine:** *worming medicine and anything else the chickens may need.*

# Small livestock

"Share your cottage garden with sheep, goats, or pigs."

BESIDES POULTRY SUCH AS CHICKENS, DUCKS, AND GEESE, IT IS possible to keep small livestock in limited outdoor spaces. Ruminant animals such as sheep and goats are popular, as they make excellent family pets and can also produce milk, cheese, yogurt, wool, mohair, and cashmere. Pigs are another fun option, although there are limited ways you can label them as "productive" without just using them for meat.

For any small livestock, you'll need a decent amount of open space so that your animals can live a healthy and happy life. Sheep are easier to keep in a paddock than goats, whose ability to climb over almost anything means they are excellent escape artists. Both, however, can have gentle temperaments that make them great to form a bond with. You can use their produce at home or share with friends and family, but be aware that any commercial enterprise can involve paperwork around food safety and animal movement. Pigs are highly intelligent animals and can make wonderful additions to any home or small farm. Just remember that their snouts and trotters are more powerful than they look, and if they're not kept securely they can easily ransack a small garden. To share your cottage garden with sheep, goats, or pigs, you will need these basics:

- ➜ **Shelter:** *hardy breeds are better suited to all weather, but all animals benefit from shelter in extreme cold and heat.*
- ➜ **Food and water:** *usually tailored to your particular breed or purpose.*
- ➜ **Medicine:** *to prevent worms, ticks, lice, and various illnesses and diseases.*
- ➜ **Halter:** *if you can get your animals used to a halter and leash, all the better.*

# Cheesemaking

"Experiment with taste and texture in one of
mankind's oldest industries."

**M**AKING YOUR OWN CHEESE IS A GREAT WAY TO SPEND A FEW
hours in the kitchen and experiment with taste and texture
in one of mankind's oldest industries, from the light, lemony
notes of soft, crumbly cheeses, to the rich, pungent aroma of a strong
blue. You don't need a huge industrial kitchen to get started—just a
stove top and a little room in the fridge.

As with all food processes, it is important to ensure everything
is clean and hygienic. Pasteurization is a common process used by
dairies to extend the shelf life of a product. It's a useful way to destroy
harmful bacteria that could produce disease or cause spoilage, without
radically altering flavor or quality. On the other hand, removing
certain bacteria from milk used to make homemade cheese can cause
the cheese to rot rather than mature, and some claim the natural
bacteria is healthy for the body. As long as the milk is fresh and your
kitchen is clean, you can experiment with both options to see which
you prefer. To get started with making your own cheese, you will need:

→ **Fresh cow, goat, or sheep
milk:** *best fresh from the
animal or from a local
farmer's market.*

→ **Rennet:** *triggers the milk to
separate into curds and whey.*

→ **Starter culture:** *provides
the cheese with the right
bacteria to form its taste,
texture, and aroma.*

→ **Sea salt, pepper, and
herbs:** *for extra flavor and
preservation.*

→ **Large cooking pot:** *enough to
hold your milk.*

→ **Food-grade thermometer:** *to
check the temperature when
pasteurizing.*

→ **Wooden spoon and colander:**
*for sieving the mixture.*

→ **Muslin cloth or tea towel:** *for
straining the curds and whey.*

→ **Cheese molds or other
containers:** *for keeping and
maturing the cheese.*

# Pottery

"Hours of meditative creativity, hands-on therapy, and best of all, a collection of beautifully wonky pots and bowls fit for any cozy cottage home."

HAVE YOU EVER FANCIED EATING SUPPER FROM YOUR OWN homemade dinner plate? Or sipping coffee from a mug thrown on your own pottery wheel? Pottery is a popular home-based hobby and one that offers hours of meditative creativity, hands-on therapy, and best of all, a collection of beautifully wonky pots and bowls fit for any cozy cottage home. If you haven't tried much clay work before, you could invest in some polymer or air-dry clay, which doesn't need any special equipment to dry but will not produce anything as robust as a proper kiln. It will, however, allow you to get to know the material and experiment with a few shapes before investing in the equipment needed to make and fire pottery at home.

There are many different ways of working with clay, but the pottery wheel is often considered the most efficient and consistent. It takes time to learn how to use a wheel, so it's worth joining a local class to get to grips with it. To fire your clay you'll need a kiln, usually powered by wood, gas, or electricity. A brand new kiln can set you back a few hundred dollars, but there are plenty of secondhand options available online and through local community groups. Aside from a wheel and kiln, the most important thing to consider is having enough space. Pottery can be messy, and the kiln will need to be kept in an outbuilding due to the high temperature. You will need:

- **Potter's wheel:** *used to shape round ceramic ware such as plates and vases.*
- **Kiln:** *located in a garage or outbuilding due to extremely high temperatures.*
- **Cutoff wire:** *for removing pottery from the wheel.*
- **Sponge and chamois leather:** *for wetting and smoothing the pot.*
- **Pottery glaze:** *in a matte or gloss finish.*

# Index

# Image credits

Cover © Anna Krawczykowska. **2** © Anna Krawczykowska. **4-5** Annie Spratt/Unsplash. **7** © Anna Krawczykowska. **8** Lena Mytchyk/Unsplash. **11** © Anna Krawczykowska. **12** Ebba Thoresson/Unsplash. **14-15** the_burtons/Getty Images. **17** Frances Gunn/Unsplash. **18** Elin Manon. **19** Luisa Brimble/Unsplash. **21** Sixteen Miles Out/Unsplash. **22** Elin Manon. **25** Andreas Strandman/Unsplash. **26** Tamara Schipchinskaya/Unsplash. **27** Elin Manon. **28** Holly Jolliffe. **31** Simon Upton/The Interior Archive; architects Hackett Holland. **32** Annie Spratt/Unsplash. **34-35** Holly Jolliffe. **37** Lil Artsy/Unsplash. **38** Holly Jolliffe. **40** Alla Home Vintage/Unsplash. **43** © living4media/House of Pictures/Örnberg, Anna. **44-45** Elin Manon. **47** Peter Bucks/Unsplash. **48** Dawn Johnson/Unsplash. **51** © Anna Krawczykowska. **52** Holly Jolliffe. **53** Elin Manon. **55** Holly Jolliffe. **56** Elin Manon. **57** Holly Jolliffe. **58** Holly Jolliffe. **60** © living4media/Narratives/Eltes, Polly. **62-63** Holly Jolliffe. **65** © living4media/Narratives/Sanderson, Robert. **67** © living4media/Ekblom, Ulrika. **68** Jessica Delp/Unsplash. **69** Elin Manon. **71** © living4media/Möller, Cecilia. **73** Katharina Bill/Unsplash. **74** Elin Manon. **76** Elin Manon. **77** Elin Manon. **79** Annie Spratt/Unsplash. **80** Elin Manon. **81** Elin Manon. **82** © Anna Krawczykowska. **84-85** Holly Jolliffe. **87** © Anna Krawczykowska. **88 top left** Icons8 Team/Unsplash. **88 top right** Carmen Tehillah/Unsplash. **88 bottom left** Eugenivy Now/Unsplash. **88 bottom right** Clem Onojeghuo/Unsplash. **91** © living4media/Guth Linse, Tine. **92** © living4media/Narratives/Birch, Jonathan. **95** Allison Christine/Unsplash. **97** © living4media/Fröhlich, Heidi. **99** Tyler McRobert/Unsplash. **101** Elin Manon. **102** Elin Manon. **104** Annie Spratt/Unsplash. **106-107** Holly Jolliffe. **109** Annie Spratt/Unsplash. **110 top left** Irina Iriser/Unsplash. **110 top right** Camille Brodard/Unsplash. **110 bottom left** Stephanie Moody/Unsplash. **110 bottom right** Annie Spratt/Unsplash. **113** Kelly Neil/Unsplash. **114** JannHuizenga/iStock by Getty Images. **115** Franzi Meyer/Unsplash. **116** David Holifield/Unsplash. **119** Jonathan Kemper/Unsplash. **121** Sincerely Media/Unsplash. **122** Annie Spratt/Unsplash. **125** Elin Manon. **127** Vera De/Unsplash. **128** Monika Grabkowska/Unsplash. **129** Elin Manon. **130** © StockFood/Sass, Achim. **131** © StockFood/Tina Engel. **132** Annie Spratt/Unsplash. **134-135** Annie Spratt/Unsplash. **137** Annie Spratt/Unsplash. **138** Greg Rosenke/Unsplash. **141** Elin Manon. **143** Danny Shives/Unsplash. **144** Adrian Pelletier/Unsplash. **146-147** Elin Manon. **149** Tracey Hocking/Unsplash. **150** © living4media/Filipinski, Jelena. **152** Holly Jolliffe. **154-155** Holly Jolliffe. **157** Emma Dau/Unsplash. **159** Holly Jolliffe. **161** Annie Spratt/Unsplash. **162** Davide Baraldi/Unsplash. **165** Annie Spratt/Unsplash. **166** Nicolas Messifet/Unsplash. **169** © living4media/Chiaratti, Ilaria. **170** © living4media/Syl Loves. **173** Richard Lee/Unsplash. **175** Camille Brodard/Unsplash. **176** Annie Spratt/Unsplash. **178-179** Ebba Thoresson/Unsplash. **180** Bee Naturalles/Unsplash. **183** Tom Ungerer/Unsplash. **184** Annie Spratt/Unsplash. **187** © StockFood/Are Media. **189** Social Income/Unsplash.